PELICAN BOOKS
Economics of the Real World

Peter Donaldson was born in Manchester in 1934 but left shortly afterwards for Kent, where he went to Gillingham Grammar School and won an open scholarship to Balliol. He read politics, philosophy, and economics, and graduated from Oxford in 1956. He then taught very briefly in a secondary modern school and for two years in a college of technology before taking up a university appointment at Leeds. He was a lecturer in the department of economics at Leicester University 1959–62, when he also did a good deal of work for the Leicester and Nottingham University adult education departments and for the Workers' Educational Association.

At the end of 1962, he was one of the first British university teachers to be seconded to key positions in underdeveloped countries under the scheme for Commonwealth Educational Cooperation. He was appointed, for two years, as Visiting Reader in Economics at the Osmania University, Hyderabad, and subsequently extended his stay in India to four years.

In 1967 he returned to England to teach at Ruskin College, Oxford, where he is now Senior Tutor in Economics. In recent years he has done a considerable amount of broadcasting including two series for radio, two for B.B.C. television and one for I.T.V. His many books include *Guide to the British Economy*, *Worlds Apart*, *10 × Economics*, *A Question of Economics*, which has been made into a Channel 4 Series and, with John Farquhar, *Understanding the British Economy*. All of these titles are published in Penguins.

He is married and has three children.

D0767411

Peter Donaldson

Economics of the Real World

Third edition

Penguin Books

PENGUIN BOOKS

Published by the Penguin Group
27 Wrights Lane, London W8 5TZ, England
Viking Penguin Inc., 40 West 23rd Street, New York, New York 10010, USA
Penguin Books Australia Ltd, Ringwood, Victoria, Australia
Penguin Books Canada Ltd, 2801 John Street, Markham, Ontario, Canada L3R 1B4
Penguin Books (NZ) Ltd, 182–190 Wairau Road, Auckland 10, New Zealand

Penguin Books Ltd, Registered Offices: Harmondsworth, Middlesex, England

Published in Pelican Books 1973
Second edition 1978
Third edition 1984
10 9 8 7 6 5

Printed and bound in Great Britain by
Cox & Wyman Ltd, Reading
Filmset in Monophoto Plantin

Contents

Preface

The paternity of *Economics of the Real World* changed while it was in an embryonic form. Initially sired by Penguins, it became a joint publication with the B.B.C. as a result of my subsequent involvement with the television series of the same title. This meant some modification of the original conception: it seemed sensible to give it a structure which fitted in with the twenty-part television programme format, and rather more basic exposition was called for. However, although I hope the book will be useful for those who watch the series, it is still primarily intended to have an existence independent of it.

It is written for those non-economists and introductory students of economics who may have been put off by various aspects of the subject: its jargon and mystique, its unreality and lack of concern with people and their problems. The aim is to give the reader a simple account of some of the main elements of economics, to draw together various strands of criticism of both economics and economic policy, and to try to bring out into the open the underlying values of our economic system which everyone is qualified to discuss – matters like the old-fashioned but still unresolved issues of inequality and unfairness with which much of the book is concerned.

My thanks are due to a number of people. Peter Wright, chief editor of Penguins, in his loyalty and dedication is an author's ideal publisher. Bernard Adams and Chris Jelley, my producers for the television series, were immensely helpful – both in their 'nitpicking' at a draft stage and in bringing to bear a general perspective. Their curiosity about the content of the later chapters while I was still wrestling with the early ones seemed at the time premature (although necessary for their programme planning); in fact, of course, it was invaluable to have been forced to think out the overall structure at that early stage. To Robert Albury, also of the B.B.C., I am very grateful for research and preparation of tables and figures which he masterfully accomplished with his usual languid efficiency.

I am indebted to all those, mentioned in the text or not, whose work I have as usual shamelessly drawn upon. Also to Sandra Wilson who typed the final manuscript with almost alarming speed and competence.

Finally, an apology. For the second year running I have imposed on my family the absences, irritations and general gloom involved in writing to a demanding deadline. Even the dog has suffered. To Sheila and Sally, Adam and Amanda – my love, thanks and a promise that it won't happen again. At least for a while.

Preface to Second Edition

The timing of the first edition of this book was ill-judged, written as it was just 'pre-oil' (the O.P.E.C. price rises and the exploitation of the North Sea reserves). Much of the factual content therefore became dated even more rapidly than writers about the economy have come to expect. However, the 'real world' of the values which underlie our economic system has not much changed, and I have not, therefore, thought it necessary to alter the structure of the book. This is simply an up-dating. In this process, I am grateful for the valuable and highly competent assistance I have received from my colleague, Denis Haffner.

Preface to Third Edition

The six years since the second edition have witnessed quite remarkable changes in the economic scene – the effects of a world recession in which Britain suffered particularly acutely *and* a counter-revolution in economic thinking and policy.

These have necessitated much more than an updating of the text, although, in the process of restructuring and introducing new material, I have tried to retain as much of the original content as possible. I am deeply appreciative of the substantial help I have received from Alain Anderton, who approached his part of the task with great professionalism.

I am not sure about the wisdom of attempting a revised edition that blends the old and the new in this way, or how far it has been successfully achieved. What I *am* certain of is that at no time since *Economics of the Real World* first appeared has the need for awareness of the *values* underlying economic theories and decisions been greater than today. If we are to move towards a less equal and more divided society, it should be as the result of a conscious and informed choice – rather than because of a belief that there is no alternative, or that we are in the grip of economic forces which are somehow beyond our control.

I

Economists and the Economy

Economics isn't very easy to get on with. Nor, for the most part, are its practitioners. Most people are still rather nervous of economists. They view them with an uneasy mixture of awe at their authority and a growing suspicion that in fact economists may not be very good at dealing with the real problems which face us.

But for the non-economist it is difficult to be sure. While general elections are won and lost on what are ostensibly economic issues, ordinary voters have to make up their minds in almost total economic darkness. They may hold emphatic views, but these are generally based on economic folklore – a bundle of misconceptions, fallacies and superstition. Even the well-informed, prepared to air their knowledgeable opinions on most other topics under the sun, will cheerfully confess ignorance when it comes to economics.

Such widespread economic illiteracy is really rather serious. Today a modicum of economic knowledge is a vital part of political education. But surprisingly little effort has been made to impart any understanding of economic issues to the general public. At schools and colleges economics is for the specialists. The mass media tend to discuss such matters at a level of comfortable superficiality. And economists themselves have shown little interest in sharing their secrets with outsiders. They have generally preferred to maintain the mystique of their discipline by talking in a mandarin jargon which only the initiated can hope to understand. Indeed, so uncommunicative are economists as a breed that they have the greatest difficulty in talking to each other.

Economics under Fire

Lacking the technical armoury with which to stand up to the economists on their own ground, laymen can only voice vague doubts about what it is that economists are up to. But in recent years the doubts have become stronger. More and more people *are* asking why, when there is greater economic expertise in government than ever before, does the economy still fail to work as we want it to? Students, perhaps lacking the mature sophistication to see the Emperor's clothes, sometimes ungratefully challenge the economic gospel with the gibe that it is nothing more than a defence of a bourgeois dreamworld. But most impressive of all is the increasing rumble of self-questioning from within the economic establishment itself.

For Joan Robinson, for example, then Professor of Economics at Cambridge, the writing on the wall was very clear indeed, when in December 1971 she warned her fellow-economists: 'The cranks and critics flourish because orthodox economists have neglected the great problems which everyone else feels to be urgent and menacing.' Arguing that economics was now in a state of acute crisis, she pointed to a particularly disturbing area of economists' neglect – the fundamental question of income distribution. Her conclusion was: 'We have nothing to say on the subject which above all others occupies the minds of people whom economics is supposed to enlighten.'[1]

In a 1972 edition of the *Economic Journal*, the official organ of the Royal Economic Society, *two* articles by eminent economists were devoted to criticizing the present state of economics and its lack of recent progress. Professor Phelps Brown, of London University, entitled his Presidential Address to the Society 'The Underdevelopment of Economics', and took as his starting point 'the smallness of the contribution that the most conspicuous developments of economics in the last quarter of a century have made to the most pressing problems of our times'. G. D. N. Worswick, Director of the National Institute

1. J. Robinson, 'The Second Crisis of Economic Theory', *American Economics Association Papers and Proceedings*, May 1972, p. 8.

of Economic and Social Research, asking 'Is Progress in Economic Science Possible?', also expressed his uneasiness. 'The standards are high, the intellectual battalions are powerful, but notwithstanding the appearance of formidable progress in techniques of all kinds the performance of economics seems curiously disappointing, the moment one puts a few test questions.' The first of Mr Worswick's test questions was simply – what are the causes of inflation in the United Kingdom at the present time?

The charge against economists is, above all, that of irrelevance. Economics, to the outsider, might seem an inherently earthy study rooted firmly in the worldly stuff of everyday life. But the world about which economists have commonly woven their theories has generally been one of their own making, remote from reality itself. There are two main reasons for this.

The first stems from the technical immaturity of the subject. The study of economics is still a relatively new one. Although quite a lot of progress has been made in understanding how the economy works, the areas of economic ignorance – questions to which economists should honestly answer 'We simply don't know' – are far more widespread than the general public (and sometimes governments) usually think. There are too few economists prepared to agree with Professor Phelps Brown that 'our own science has hardly reached its seventeenth century'.[2]

Faced with the problem of explaining a complex reality, the economist's approach is to reduce that reality to a simplified 'model' which can be more easily handled. In itself, such a method is perfectly proper. But in economics it has often had disastrous consequences. Having built up a model in the first place, economists have proved very reluctant ever to modify or replace it. The result is that what may once have been a rough representation of the real world becomes, after a time, nothing but a theoretical abstraction; its abstruseness in the face of major structural and institutional changes is increasingly

2. E. H. Phelps Brown, 'The Underdevelopment of Economics', *Economic Journal*, March 1972, p. 10.

evident to students of the subject. Worse still is the way in which economists, having deduced how things would work in the pretend-world of their own models, then treat their theories as proven economic truths and suggest that they can be applied wholesale in the real world of economic policy. They have often been wrong. 'The consistently indifferent performance in practical application is in fact a symptom of the fundamental imbalance of our discipline. The weak and all too slowly growing empirical foundation clearly cannot support the proliferating superstructure of pure, or should I say speculative, economic theory.'[3]

Apart from its technical immaturity, there is a more profound reason why economics is accused of being remote from the real world. Many economists claim to be scientists just as much as physicists or chemists are, though they have a special handicap in being unable to perform laboratory experiments. Now adherence to scientific principles is a very good thing if it means simply that economists recognize that they must submit their hypotheses to rigorous testing before they elevate them to the status of accepted knowledge. In fact, however, this discipline of scientific method is not something which economists have shown much interest in; on the contrary, nearly every introductory economics text is brimful of untested hypotheses passing as received economic theory. No, it is a quite different aspect of the scientific imprimatur which principally appeals to economists. As scientists, they claim to study what *is* rather than what *ought* to be. They can make statements with *objective* authority – as distinct from the value-ridden propositions of politicians and the rest. Theirs are purely technical conclusions derived from detached, impartial analysis, only at a later stage sullied and muddied by the value judgements of those who are responsible for acting upon them or who feel their consequences.

In fact, economics is far from value-free. Bias appears both in selection of the questions deemed to be legitimate subjects

3. W. Leontief, 'Theoretical Assumptions and Non-observed Facts', *American Economic Review*, 1971, p. 1.

of economic analysis and in the ways in which those questions are treated. Issues of economic justice, for example, are considered non-scientific, while at the same time something like 'free competition' can be analysed with an apparent impartiality which conceals the fact, as Myrdal puts it, that proof of its theoretical effectiveness transforms it into a 'political desideratum'.

Economics claims to be value-free and is nothing of the sort. But its pseudo-scientific pretensions set it apart from the real world of emotions, values and prejudices from which it tries to remain aloof. Economics and economic policy cannot be devoid of values if they are to be taken as serious attempts to cope with the problems of the world in which we live. The matters which concern people – questions of where they stand in relation to others, the nature of their working conditions, the quality of life in its many aspects – these are the real issues which economics can neglect only at peril of becoming totally irrelevant. To be of any help, economists *have* to begin from a set of values and be prepared to use their analysis instrumentally, in revealing, not just how the economy works now, but also how it ought to work. Economists are not, however, philosopher-kings. They have no *special* right to dictate how society should behave and be governed. But they have as much right as anyone else. And if they are to be concerned with issues most relevant to the real world, then the value-content of economics must be declared rather than denied.

Why Economists Disagree

To outsiders, one of the main factors undermining the credibility of economists is their notorious inability to agree about anything at all. But, given the nature and limitations of economics which we have just been discussing, the failure of economists to speak with a single voice is easily explicable. Only *if* economics were the mature, objective science which it pretends to be – only *if* it consisted of a body of proven, value-free theories – could we expect different economists always to come to similar conclusions. Since it is not that at all, the lack of agreement among economists is inevitable.

Take, for example, the question of whether Britain should have joined Europe. During the 1960s, one of the major policy issues about which governments and the public turned to economists for expert advice was the vexed question of whether or not Britain should join the six members of the European Economic Community. In the course of the 'Great Debate' of that time, Professor Kaldor of Cambridge University organized a letter to *The Times* opposing British entry. The letter was signed by no less than 153 academic and business economists. A few days later, another letter was published in *The Times* supporting British membership of the E.E.C. and signed by 141 professional economists.

How could this come about? How could the profession be split down the middle on an issue about which non-economists might reasonably expect clear guidance from the experts?

Partly it was the result of sheer technical ignorance. Economics could provide no clear-cut answers to the questions of what the static advantages and disadvantages of British entry would be – the effects of increased specialization and trade between members of an enlarged Community – or about the dynamic effects of increased scale of production, of greater mobility of labour and capital, and of joining a bloc with a record of faster economic growth than Britain. Even the direction of the changes which would follow British entry was uncertain, let alone when their impact would be felt or how great it would be. Economists simply didn't know. But that unfortunately did not deter them from making firm, albeit widely different, predictions.

Beyond that, the division in economic opinion stemmed from the quite different value-premises on which the two groups based their analysis. Thus some supported British entry because they saw in a wider Europe a strengthening of western capitalism against economic and political threats from within and without. Others opposed it on precisely the same grounds. But this was no simple split between 'left-wing' and 'right-wing' economists.

Because nobody knew what the consequences would be (although they often thought that they did) it was equally possible for both left and right to come to the conclusion that Britain should join Europe – or for them both to parade under the Anti-Market banner.

By the early eighties the argument was still raging, although the question was now whether or not Britain should leave the E.E.C. This time there was more 'evidence' available. We now know what has happened to the British economy in more than a decade of community membership. But even this mass of data does not lead to unanimity among economists because of their ability to interpret the data in infinitely differing ways. The problem lies in isolating the 'E.E.C. effect', in deciding how far what has happened, for example, to the balance of payments or to the rate of economic growth, has been as a result of Community membership or in spite of it. Even if it were true that the British economy had suffered as a result of E.E.C. membership, it would still not be possible to conclude that withdrawal would improve its performance. The experience of the second decade of community membership may be very different from the first. And underlying differences of political values continue to divide economists on the relative importance to be placed on different aspects of the evidence.

Determining whether or not Britain has been or would be better-off inside or outside the E.E.C. is admittedly a vast and multifaceted issue. But if we take an apparently more straight-forward question, such as 'What causes inflation?', laymen are surely entitled to expect that here at least economists could speak with a single voice and offer an unequivocal view about a matter which seems so clearly to be within their own technical province.

Alas, it is not so. For most of the post-war period there was argument between economists about whether rising prices were due to excessive spending in the economy or to the pressure of rising costs such as wages. The past decade has seen a more fundamental controversy about the role of the money supply in the process. By the late 1970s, it was the 'monetarists' who had won the day in persuading government that tight regulation of the money supply was the key to price stability.

We shall be examining the nature of inflation in a subsequent chapter. For the time being the interesting point is that in March 1981, at a time when monetarism was fully dominating government thinking and policy, no less than 364 university economists saw fit to issue a statement attacking its fundamental tenets.

As with the argument about the E.E.C., the source of disagreement between economists fell into three broad categories.

(i) A dispute about the facts of the matter – just what did the statistics show about the relationship between inflation and its possible causes?

(ii) An inability to resolve the dispute by a controlled experiment in which the effects of each of the principal determinants could be clearly isolated.

(iii) An underlying disagreement of values about the relative priority that should be given to conflicting objectives of policy, like controlling inflation and avoiding unemployment.

Unfortunately, on nearly every main aspect of economic policy, we shall encounter similar deep divisions of economic opinion. For the non-economist it is more than merely confusing. Millions of ordinary lives may be blighted by decisions taken on the basis of suspect economic 'expertise'.

It may seem somewhat perverse to introduce a subject by harping on its inadequacies. But if Leontief is right in saying that 'Economics today rides the crest of intellectual respectability and popular acclaim', and that 'The serious attention with which our pronouncements are received by the general public, hard-bitten politicians, and even sceptical businessmen is second only to that which was given to physicists and space experts a few years ago when the round trip to the moon seemed to be our only truly national goal',[4] then it is important that we should be fully aware of the limitations of economics. Economists cannot always be relied upon to remind us of them,

4. Leontief, op. cit.

although, as we have seen, there are some who are acutely aware that their discipline is in a state of crisis.

Economists and Economic Policy

Despite the manifest inadequacies and limitations of economics, governments do act on economic advice. A chancellor faced with conflicting advice may choose to follow his own paid advisers – Treasury economists in the British case – or he may be influenced by economists outside the government circle. More likely, he will impose his own value-judgements on the expert opinion to produce his particular brand of economic policy. Whatever he does, his thinking will be constrained by his understanding of what economic theorists are saying, or have said. John Maynard Keynes once suggested, indeed, that every practical politician is, on close inspection, a 'slave of some defunct economist'.

During the post-war period the bondage has been highly explicit. For the years from 1945 to the mid-1970s it was the ideas of one dead economist – John Maynard Keynes himself – which provided the theoretical framework within which government policies of 'managing the economy' were based. Since that time, it has been monetarism, a much older school of thought than Keynesianism, which has come increasingly to re-dominate economic thinking.

The post-war decades have seen changes not only in the nature of economic policies adopted by governments, but also in the objectives for which those policies have been used. Until the early 1970s, there was a clear consensus that the first objective of policy was the achievement of a high and stable level of employment. In addition, governments aimed to secure price stability, economic growth and a sound balance of payments. During more recent years, however, there has been a remarkable abandonment of full employment as the main policy goal, with control of inflation replacing it as the priority.

In subsequent chapters, we shall be examining the means by which governments have attempted to achieve their various objectives and how far economics has contributed to the process. This will involve a preliminary look in Chapter 2 at the major symptom of our present economic plight – unemployment – followed by more detailed examination of alternative economic theories and attempts to apply them. We shall see that immediate economic policy objectives were to a great extent achieved until the onslaught of the explosive inflation during the early and mid-1970s. However, subsequent measures to deal with rising prices have been successful only at a massive cost in terms of other policy objectives. This has resulted from a failure to adapt Keynesianism – the framework of economic thought once used with so much apparent success – to deal with new economic circumstances, such as the 'stagflation' of the mid-1970s. Instead, there has been an espousal of the monetarist creed – with far-reaching consequences.

But when this is done, even more significant questions will remain unanswered. The theme of this book is that the so-called 'ends' of economic policy – whether they be full employment, rapid economic growth, balance of payments equilibrium, or price stability – are nothing of the sort. Important though they may be (particularly when they are not being achieved), they are the means rather than the ends. Far more fundamental are the issues that lie behind them.

Thus it is not just a matter of securing full employment, but also of questioning – jobs for whom, where, and performed in what conditions?

Similarly, the 'rate of economic growth' is of no real concern to you or me; what matters is what is happening to our standard of living, what an increase in national output is made up of, and the cost to ourselves and our environment of achieving it. Above all, perhaps, we are concerned with the issue of equity – whether or not the economic system is working fairly. The distribution of income and wealth, how much we get and have by comparison with others, occupies a central place in most people's thoughts about economics.

This is the stuff of the real world. It is a world apart from that of economic statistics, exchange rates, stock-market valuations and the Gross National Product (G.N.P.). The real world is often incapable of precise measurement; it is not a clinical laboratory in which economic experiments can be carefully conducted. It is a world of which prejudices and values are an inextricable part rather than a veneer which must be delicately removed and set aside before objective analysis can begin. For that reason it is a world which economics has largely neglected.

2

Unemployment: the Great Divide

The headlines regularly announce further recruits to the army of the unemployed, already more than three million strong. Long-established firms are contracting, laying off workers, or crashing altogether. There seems no end to the crisis, with occasional splutters of recovery quickly petering out. Of course, the economy has been in difficulties for over a decade now but these seem dwarfed by comparison with the present dimensions of the problem. Politicians express deep concern for the unfortunate victims of unemployment but offer little immediate hope for alleviating their plight. Many economists say that workers have priced themselves out of jobs, some even that unemployment benefits need to be cut to encourage workers more actively to seek work. Others argue that unemployment is caused by a lack of demand in the economy. Massive technological change is also seen as threatening job prospects. The orthodox view is that free market forces will, if left alone, provide the answers. Others argue that only massive state intervention can bring about a solution to a problem caused by the free market mechanism. The time is 1932.

Fifty years on, nothing seems to have changed. Unemployment has once again reached appalling levels. Once again, a generation of youngsters is faced with the prospect of years of uncertain, irregular employment. Those in jobs consider themselves to be fortunate. Once again, there is no consensus among economists and politicians about how to solve our problems, but instead a deep division of opinion about their causes and cures. Before examining those divisions, we will look first at the seriousness of unemployment. Who are the unemployed, and to what extent is unemployment a genuine cost to society?

Defining unemployment is not as simple as it might seem. Take for instance the commonsense definition that the unemployed are those 'actively seeking work who are not at present in paid employment'. This is likely to underestimate the extent of unemployment for two reasons. First, many people not actively seeking work would nonetheless like a job if it were easily available. But in times of high unemployment, they realize that actively looking for work is likely to be fruitless. Second, many people in part-time employment would like to secure a full-time job, but this preference is concealed by the official statistics which include them as already in employment.

Until 1982, the unemployment figures in Britain were based on a count of all those registered as unemployed at jobcentres and unemployment offices. The assumption was that such registration indicated an active search for work on the part of the unemployed individual. But as we have argued, this figure underestimated unemployment because many unemployed did not bother to register. It also overestimated unemployment since some of those registered were not in fact interested in getting another job. This arose because registration at a jobcentre was a condition for collecting unemployment benefit. Among those doing so was a growing number of men and women who had taken early retirement and who were registering only to be able to claim national insurance credits – vital for their old age pension.

In October 1982, the government changed the method of calculating unemployment in Britain. Instead of counting those registered at jobcentres, it now only counts those who claim unemployment benefit as a result of being jobless. The result was the disappearance of nearly 200,000 unemployed people from the count in that month. In addition, some 200,000 over-sixties were subsequently excluded by decisions that they would no longer have to sign on to receive unemployment benefit or to receive national insurance credits. Also excluded are more than half a million on government make-work schemes – such as the Youth Training programme. So are the 250,000 women that the Department of Employment itself admits are seeking work but are not claiming benefit. It is easy to see why some claim that the official unemployment falls short of the true figure by more than a million.

Moreover, these are national figures. Unemployment does not affect all parts of the community equally. If you are sixteen and living in Newcastle-upon-Tyne, your chances of having a job are virtually zero. In 1983, you were almost twice as likely to be unemployed if you lived in the North of England as in the South-East of England. Nearly one in five workers was unemployed in Northern Ireland, the worst affected region in the U.K.

Unskilled general labourers and coloured people are another two groups particularly hard hit. A managerial or professional white male aged thirty-five living in the South-East of England is unlikely to remain unemployed for long. A coloured female general labourer aged eighteen living in Glasgow will be very lucky to keep any type of steady employment.

If the scale of unemployment is worse than the official statistics suggest, is the cost involved also greater than it might at first seem? Unemployment affects the vast majority of people in society. The worst hit are of course the unemployed themselves. They are likely to suffer a major drop in their take-home income. The more they earn before losing their job, the more they stand to lose from unemployment. Of course, a few of those unemployed are better-off on the dole than in any job they are likely to get. But despite all the publicity given to this group of people, they are unlikely to form more than a small proportion of the unemployed, certainly less than 10 per cent. For the other 90 per cent, unemployment means penally low living standards. The dole is not a generous hand-out: in 1981, for example, flat-rate unemployment benefit equalled only 32 per cent of net average earnings. For the long-term unemployed, even with supplementary benefit, the future prospect is one of penny-pinching poverty.

The unemployed face not only a loss of earnings but also

a variety of hidden costs. On average they are more likely to live in substandard housing and to suffer illness. Depression, violence and alcoholism are other conditions associated with unemployment. And yet society at large, in referring to the unemployed, at best sees them as 'deserving cases' or 'victims of the economic situation'. At worst, they are labelled 'scroungers', 'workshy', 'failures' and 'layabouts'.

But the rest of society also suffers from unemployment. Financially, it is those in work who have to meet the huge bill that is entailed. Two independent studies published in 1981, one by the Manpower Services Commission,[1] the other by the Institute of Fiscal Studies,[2] showed that the cost to the taxpayer of each unemployed person was between £4,400 and £4,500 a year. Only about one-third of this sum represented benefits and other welfare payments received by the unemployed. The other two-thirds represented the income tax, national insurance contributions and indirect taxes which the government would have received if the unemployed had remained at work. Not only do the employed have to pay for the benefits for the jobless: they also have to make good the tax 'loss' resulting from mass unemployment. By 1983, the estimated cost of 3 million unemployed to the government was about £15,000m.,[3] the equivalent of just under £300 for every man, woman and child in the country. If there had been no unemployment, the government could have halved the standard rate of income tax, or abolished V.A.T. or more than doubled spending on the National Health Service.

Unemployment, then, represents a highly expensive as well as ugly blot on our society. Why on earth then do we tolerate scarce resources lying idle at a time when consumers are crying out for more goods and services to buy? How does mass

1. Manpower Services Commission, *Review of Services for the Unemployed*, 1981.

2. A. Dilnot and C. Morris, 'The Exchequer Cost of Unemployment', *Fiscal Studies* (2), November 1981.

3. Based upon figures from the House of Lords, *Report of the Select Committee on Unemployment*, 1982.

unemployment arise? Is there really nothing that governments can do about it?

As we shall see, economists are deeply divided in their analysis. For the remainder of this chapter we take a preliminary look at two broad views about the causes of unemployment: that it is the result of wages being too high – and that it is due to lack of demand in the economy.

Too High Wages?

The orthodoxy of the 1980s is, surprisingly, the very orthodoxy of the 1930s which seemed for a long period to have been thoroughly discredited. It is the view that the level of unemployment in an economy depends essentially on the *wage rate* – which in turn is the result of the forces of supply and demand in the labour market. The argument runs as follows.

By and large, it is safe to generalize that the higher the wage rate, the more workers will offer themselves for hire. Firms, on the other hand, will see matters differently. For them, the higher the wage rate, the fewer workers they are prepared to take on. Taking three possible wage rates – £50, £100 and £150 a week – the amount of labour on offer and the amount of jobs which firms would be prepared to offer might be as in Table 1.

Table 1

Wage rate	Supply of labour	Jobs offered
£50	250	750
£100	500	500
£150	750	250

Precisely the same information can be shown in a graphical form (Fig. 1).

What becomes clear is that there is only *one* wage rate at which the amount of labour coming onto the market is compatible with the amount of jobs which the firms are willing to create. That 'equilibrium' wage rate is obviously £100 a week. At £150, the supply of labour will exceed the demand

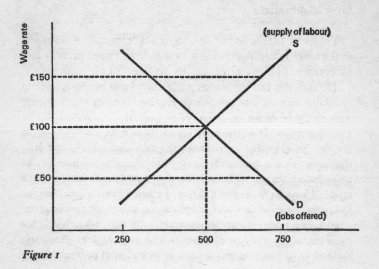

Figure 1

for it; at £50, the number of jobs offered will be greater than the number of people offering themselves for hire.

When we talk of unemployment, we generally refer to that which is involuntary – people without jobs who would be willing to accept work at the going rate. Provided that wage rates are flexible, unemployment in this sense should exist only temporarily, as a result of the wage rate rising above the equilibrium level. As soon as the excess of supply over demand forces it down again, the market for labour will clear itself in just the same way that the market for oranges does.

This is just what the majority of economists were saying in the 1930s. The dreadful unemployment of that time, they argued, arose principally because wage rates were too high. If only they could be cut, there would be jobs for everyone who wanted them. And what stopped them falling naturally was the existence of a major imperfection in the labour market – trade unions, which, in trying to maintain an artificially high wage rate, succeeded only in limiting the number of jobs which firms could create.

This was the belief of the so-called 'classical' economists in the early 1930s. And it remains the view of their present-day successors, who are often loosely referred to as 'monetarists' – although this is a somewhat misleading label because, strictly speaking, monetarism refers to an economic theory which argues that the sole cause of inflation is excessive increases in the money supply. It is the analysis of these modern disciples of the free market that constitutes the new orthodoxy, and it is the same as the old orthodoxy: that if unemployment is to be reduced, wage levels must be cut. And just as in the 1930s trade unions were seen as a major obstacle to this happening, so today trade unions are accused of having too much power at the negotiating table. By achieving artificially high wage levels for their members, they price other workers out of jobs. Breaking the power of trade unions is seen as an essential prerequisite of a return to full employment.

On top of that, it is frequently argued that unemployment benefits should be reduced to a level that increases the incentive to seek work – by making acceptance of lower-paid jobs a more attractive proposition.

During the 1930s, classical or monetarist policies were implemented. Trade-union power was weakened as unemployment broke the militancy that had characterized much of the 1920s. Unemployment benefits were cut and the government gave the lead to the private sector by cutting those wage incomes under its own direct control. The 'Geddes Axe' chopped the incomes of teachers, the armed forces and the civil services. However, the policies did not work, and unemployment remained a serious problem throughout the thirties. And yet, despite the apparent failure of these policies, fifty years on they are once again being tried. Labour bargaining strength is again reduced by the threat of unemployment, and legislation since 1974 has been designed further to curb union power. Governments have also attempted to reduce public-sector wages in the hope that the private sector would follow suit. Unemployment benefits have been cut, at least for the first six months of a period of unemployment. Just as in the 1930s, these measures seem to have made little impact on the unemployment figures.

Advocates of the view that the labour market will 'clear' itself if left free to do so might claim that unemployment persisted in the 1930s and does so again today because of a *failure* adequately to reduce average real wages. But there are also reasons for believing that even if it were feasible, such a policy would not in fact work.

That is because the case may be an example of the 'fallacy of composition' – the erroneous belief that what is true for the parts must necessarily be true for the whole.

Thus for the individual firm, wage cuts *might* have the desired effect. A cut in wage-rates might, if the firm was boldly optimistic about its prospects, represent a reduction in costs sufficient to induce it to produce more and employ additional workers. But if *all* wages were cut at the same time, spending in the economy would be correspondingly reduced; the purchasing power to buy the increased output simply wouldn't be there. As Joan Robinson once put it, the effect is analogous to the man going to watch a procession who takes with him a box to stand on. If he is the only one who does so, he will get a better view. But if everyone takes along a box, they are back where they started from.

It can be argued that against this must be set the extra orders stemming from wealth-owners in society – who, because prices have been falling, are now better-off than before – and from overseas customers attracted by the cheap price of British exports. But it is unlikely that these will outweigh the loss of business from the British workers who have either seen their wages reduced or have been made redundant.

Too Little Spending?

If cutting wages is not the answer to unemployment, then what is? Some fifty years ago an alternative was proposed. By the mid-1930s, John Maynard Keynes was finishing what he described in a letter to George Bernard Shaw as a 'book of economic theory which will largely revolutionize – not I suppose, at once, but in the course of the next ten years – the way the world thinks about economic problems'. With the publication of his *General Theory of Employment, Interest and Money* in 1936, Keynes achieved an intellectual somersault which might have converted the vicious circle of his times into a potentially virtuous one. For many years he had been struggling intuitively against economic orthodoxy before he succeeded in articulating the causes of cyclical unemployment and what it was about an unregulated market system which made recurring unemployment near-inevitable. In retrospect, it is all very simple.

The key to increased employment, argued Keynes, lay in more spending. The unemployment of the 1930s was tragically paradoxical. The workers were there, the capital was there. The workers wanted jobs, the producers wanted profit. There was no immediate conflict of interest. The missing ingredient was simply the wherewithal to buy any increase in output. *Anything*, said Keynes, which raises demand in the economy will contribute to reducing unemployment. If you like, employ men to dig holes in the ground and fill them up again. Pay them incomes. What will they do with them? They will go out and spend the greater part – on food, clothes, beer, paying bills. The recipients of such payments would, in turn, undertake further spending themselves, and a cumulative process of income expansion would begin, drawing into employment more and more hitherto unemployed resources.

Hole-digging, although it would do the trick, is an unimaginative and unproductive way of stimulating an economy. How much more sensible for the government to create incomes by spending on socially worthwhile projects like road-building or slum clearance, and ultimately to restore the confidence of private entrepreneurs. Once that happens they will invest in new factories and machines, producing goods to meet the demands of consumers whose incomes have been increased by being absorbed again into the active work-force.

But where is the money to come from to pay for such a grandiose design? It is very difficult for the non-economist (and it was also difficult for economists at that time) to realize that shortage of money can never be a constraint for governments in a modern economy. Money, although it means so much to us as individuals, is only a lubricator of the economic system; what matters is the volume of real things – goods and services – which the economy is able to produce. The money supply is in the hands of government, which can readily increase it (although, as will be argued in Chapter 5, it may be considerably more difficult for a government to hold back its rate of growth, or actually decrease it). If, in conditions of full employment, it doubles the quantity of money by handing us all out a bonus equivalent to our present incomes, we certainly won't be twice as well off as a result. When we try to spend our increased incomes, we will come across the problem that there are no more goods available in the shops. Our increased purchasing power, in those circumstancès, may merely lead to higher prices. But when there is mass unemployment, the situation is a very different one. In this case, spending a hand-out from the State soon leads to a feed-back to producers, who rush to employ labour and other resources to meet our increased demands.

What was needed, claimed Keynes, was a combination of various measures. The government could try to snap the private sector out of its depression, by offering tax cuts (to both firms and consumers), lower interest rates and subsidies of one kind and another. Or the government could undertake the job of expanding demand itself. If the private sector was sticky, the government itself should operate as the big spender, knowing that sooner or later private firms would respond to the increased market for their goods which such a policy would produce.

Stimulate the private sector, 'pump-prime' it through government spending – and, if necessary, persist with compensatory expenditure by the State to make good the deficiencies of private firms. This was the sort of package which Keynes recommended, and each of its ingredients was directly opposite to the recommendations of the orthodox economists of his day.

Such iconoclastic advice, however, went against the grain for two reasons. The first was that it was contrary to all the canons of 'sound finance' on which governmental economics had been built since the days of Gladstone. The function of the Treasury, it was held, was essentially one of good housekeeping. In the same way as you or I know that we must keep our spending in line with income if we are to avoid the attentions of the Official Receiver, so a government which disburses more than it receives in taxation will also end up in Queer Street, having meanwhile 'put the country in the red'. But this, like the argument about wage cuts, is an example of the fallacy of composition: what is true of the parts need not necessarily be true of the whole. If *you* get into debt, spend more than your income, then it will be to another individual or bank who will ultimately demand repayment and put the pressure on. But if your debt is to another member of your family, then – whatever the domestic acrimony which it causes – the family itself will be neither worse off nor better off than before. It is an internal book-keeping transaction between the members.

Similarly, if the government spends more than it receives in taxes – by, for example, borrowing from the general public – then, provided it doesn't involve foreigners, its increased indebtedness is a domestic matter between members of the national family which it represents. The economy as a whole is neither richer nor poorer than before. But if the effect of government borrowing from one section of the community to finance higher spending is that unemployment is reduced and output increased, the economy *will* be better off than before. With the higher tax revenues which will result from increased incomes, the original borrowing can, if so desired, be repaid.

Deficit financing in a depression, far from being profligate extravagance, is straightforward common sense.

The other reason why contemporaries found it so difficult to swallow the Keynesian prescription was that it represented a political attack on a hallowed orthodoxy. The essence of the Keynesian message was that a totally unregulated, *laissez-faire*, free-enterprise economy simply could not be relied upon to do the job of creating and maintaining full employment. If the degradation and sheer waste of unemployment was ever to be eliminated, the State would have to accept explicit responsibility for achieving that objective. Moreover, the means which it would have to use represented a quite unprecedented degree of interference in the everyday workings of the economy. Business could no longer be left to businessmen; what was required was a substantial circumscription of their actions, manipulation of their behaviour in order to yield the right overall result. What had been widely dubbed as 'meddling' or 'interference' in the past would now have to be sold as paternalistic intervention.

It was a bitter pill. The idea that State management of the economy was an essential means to the widely willed end of full employment was highly unpalatable. But Keynes was no Marxist extremist. 'Even if we need a religion, how can we find it in the rabid rubbish of the Red bookshops? It is hard for an educated, decent, intelligent son of Western Europe to find his ideals here, unless he has first suffered some strange and horrid process of conversion which has changed all his values.'[4] Keynes's values *hadn't* been transformed by his economic discoveries. 'I can be influenced by what seems to be justice and good sense; but the *class* war will find me on the side of the educated *bourgeoisie*.'[5] For Keynes, his theory was 'moderately conservative in its implications. For whilst it indicates the vital importance of establishing certain central controls in matters which are now left in the main to individual

4. J. M. Keynes, *Essays in Persuasion*, Macmillan, 1931
5. Ibid.

initiative, there are wide fields of activity which are unaffected.'[6] Keynes, coming as he did from the great liberal tradition, argued that a more active interventionist policy on the part of government was the only way in which that tradition could be preserved. The old order, capitalism itself, could survive only with this major modification.

Here, then, are two radically different approaches to the causes and hence cures for unemployment. There is a third view that the future impact of new technology will be so great as to make both of the others equally irrelevant. Neither wage-cutting nor demand-creation will be sufficient to avoid the very unequal distribution of the benefits of new technology in a two-nation Britain: one nation in technologically sophisticated and highly paid work, the other out of work or in low-paid service occupations. This pessimistic vision is one to which we shall give further consideration later.

But for the meantime we shall delve deeper into Keynesian theory and policy in Chapters 3 and 4, and in the two subsequent chapters outline the 'monetarist' approach that in recent years has come to replace it as the economic orthodoxy.

6. J. M. Keynes, *The General Theory of Employment, Interest and Money*, Macmillan, 1936, pp. 377–8.

3

Basic Keynes

At the heart of the Keynesian analysis is the proposition that the volume of employment in an economy depends on the amount of spending that is taking place. What is more, Keynes argued, the level of national expenditure or *demand* that is needed to buy all the goods and services that could be produced with full employment is *not* an automatic outcome of an economy left to its own devices. Indeed it is most unlikely that the actual level of national income and spending and the amount required for full employment will be identical.

So what determines the level of spending in an economy? This is a complex matter and we shall have to resort to the economist's irritating but useful trick of starting with a very simplified 'model' of the economy, and adding more realistic complications stage by stage.

Imagine, then, an economy in which there is no foreign trade (a 'closed' economy), and in which there is no governmental economic activity. In this economy, we shall focus on the behaviour of two very broad groups – households and firms. Firms are the producing units in the economy. They hire the services of people from the households, put them to work in their factories and produce goods which they then sell to households in their capacity as consumers. Households, on the other hand, are the places where people live, eat, drink and make love. They are also the source of the economy's labour supply and the purchasers of national output. The relationships between households and firms can be illustrated in a simple 'circular flow' diagram.

Fig. 2A shows the material interdependence between the two.

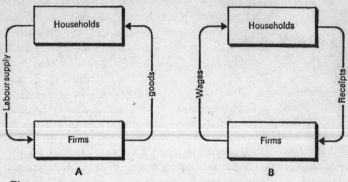

Figure 2

From households to firms, there is a flow of factor services as the working population offers itself for hire in the firms' factories. And from firms to households there is a flow of goods which the firms have produced with the help of the labour force. Corresponding to these physical flows are financial relationships between firms and households shown in Fig. 2B. These monetary flows are in the reverse direction to the physical flows. Thus there are payments, firstly from firms to households in the form of wages, and secondly from households to firms, firms' receipts resulting from the sale of their goods.

Just one more simplifying, if absurd, assumption, and we

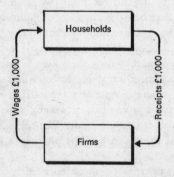

Figure 3

can put our basic economy to work. Suppose that people, when they get their wages, spend them wholly and immediately on goods – they save nothing at all. Then if the value of output produced by the firms happens to be, say, £1,000, the economy will operate as in Fig. 3.

The firms hire £1,000 of labour from the households, and pay out a wage bill of that amount. The households then use those wages to buy the output of the firms, so that the £1,000 returns to the firms in the form of receipts. It is then available to the firms to repeat the process. The £1,000 income level is self-perpetuating. (This assumes that the firms are producing the goods which people *want*. Mistakes, it is supposed, will only be temporary and soon corrected by shifts in resources between different lines of production to reflect consumers' patterns of preference.

This basic economy is one in which, if we label income Y, and consumption C, then Y = C. Its only use is to emphasize one very important point. That is, what are costs to the firms are incomes to households. Therefore, since the firms sell their output at prices which are made up of their various costs, the income of households (which are costs looked at from a different viewpoint) is always sufficient for them to buy the firms' output in its entirety. The level of income and output in this basic economy is obviously stable. There is no reason why it should ever deviate from £1,000.

Now let us drop some of the simplifying assumptions of the basic model. First of all, what difference does it make that, in practice, incomes are *not* all immediately and wholly spent on consumption? Some part is saved, put aside from a variety of motives resplendently catalogued by Keynes as: Precaution, Foresight, Calculation, Improvement, Independence, Pride and Avarice.[1]

The effect can be seen in Fig. 4.

Savings – £200 in this case – represents a leakage from the circular flow. It is £200 which does *not* return to the firms. And since the receipts of the firms are what they use to pay

1. J. M. Keynes, *General Theory of Employment, Interest and Money*, p. 108.

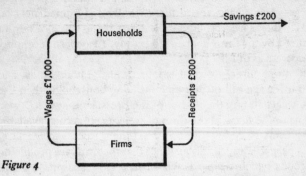

Figure 4

for workers, the number which they are able to hire is correspondingly reduced. As a result of their saving, households will thus find themselves at the next stage with reduced incomes of only £800. If their savings behaviour is stable – if, that is, we suppose that they will always try to save one fifth of their incomes – then the consequences are startling indeed. The next few stages in the process are summarized in Fig. 5, showing reduced receipts to the firms and therefore reduced incomes to the people – of £640, £512 and £409.60.

The final outcome of this process is predictable. Receipts to firms and incomes to households will fall to zero! Our attempt to explain reality has clearly overshot the mark. Things aren't *that* bad even today. To redress the balance somewhat, another complication needs to be taken into account. Savings are a leakage from the system of circular flow. But there is also an important *injection* into the flow which has so far been neglected. That is, investment.

A word of caution is needed at this point. Although economists are accused of jargonizing, they also use a large number of everyday terms. But they re-define them to serve the purpose of economic analysis and give them meaning quite different from their usual connotations. Thus 'investment' in ordinary usage means building society deposits, holdings of stocks and shares and the like. That, however, is not the meaning of the

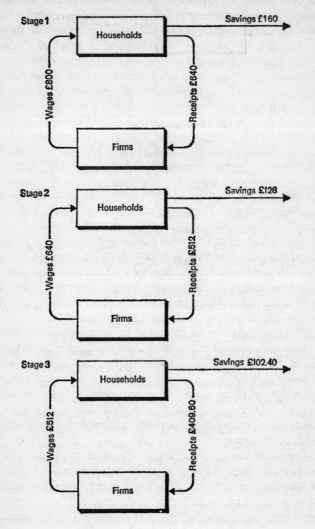

Figure 5

term in economics. For economists, investment is a *real* rather than a monetary matter. It denotes the increase, over a period of time, in the 'capital stock' – of plant, machinery, roads and so on. It is the addition to the accumulation of past output which was not consumed at the time.

In our model, investment is a further source of demand for the firms' output. So far we have assumed that the firms produce only final goods – for sale to households. In fact, however, some firms will produce *capital* goods rather than consumer goods, for sale to other firms. Therefore, in addition to consumer demand from households, firms will also be receiving orders for capital or investment goods from other firms. Investment is thus an *injection* into the circular flow of income. If, as is the case in Fig. 6, the amount of investment (£200) just matches the leakage from the system in the form of savings, then a stable level of income of £1,000 is maintained.

Such an equality between savings and investment does not seem *prima facie* very likely. The problem is that in the model, and to some extent in the real world too, savers are different people from investors and act from quite different motivations. Individuals save for a variety of reasons – for their old age, to get married, to buy a new car, to guard against a rainy day. Investment, on the other hand, is undertaken by firms intent upon building up their capacity to meet some expected increase in demand in the future and to profit from it. Since savings and investment decisions are made from different motives by different people unaware of the actions of others, there is no reason at all why what one group plan to save will be precisely matched by what the other group plan to invest. (Although there will be overlapping: firms themselves may save to finance their own investment, and to that extent the two sets of decisions are kept in line.)

The consequences of the highly probable disparity between savings and investment plans are far-reaching. If the amount which households plan to save exceeds the amount which firms plan to invest, the result will be similar to that illustrated in Fig. 4 (where savings happened to be £200 and investment

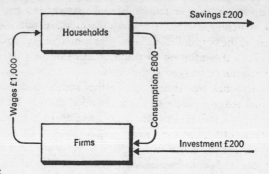

Figure 6

zero). There will be a *downward* pressure on the level of income. If, on the other hand, firms plan to invest (and do so on the basis of bank credit) more than households plan to save, the effect will be for incomes and output to be pushed up.

We therefore have all the ingredients here for an unstable economy, with income and output fluctuating in response to changing savings and investment plans.

But these upward and downward movements of income do not go on for ever. They are finite. And the way in which originally disparate plans to save and invest are ultimately made compatible is explained by the theory of the multiplier.

Suppose that, to begin with, the level of income has settled at £1,000, with savings and investment plans coincidentally equal at £200. For some reason or other, people now propose to become more thrifty. In the future they decide that they will save 25 per cent of their incomes rather than 20 per cent. Savings therefore increase to £250 in the first place (Fig. 7), and the original balance of the economy is destroyed.

What is the result? Initially, only £750 comes back to the firms as receipts, and this, together with continued investment demand of £200, is the basis of income at the next stage being reduced to £950. That, however, is not the end of the story. If, despite their lower income, people continue to try to save 25 per cent, they will set aside some £237.50 at this stage.

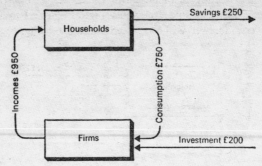

Figure 7

Consumption will consequently be reduced to £712.50 and that is the amount which returns to the firms as receipts. Added to investment demand of £200, it means that what flows back to households as incomes falls once again – to £912.50 (Fig. 8).

Income will continue to fall, but the fall at each stage is getting smaller and smaller. We can predict the final outcome. The slide in income will stop only when savings are ultimately brought into line with investment. With firms continuing to invest £200, the question which we have to ask is, 'At what level of income will people plan to save only that amount?' Since we have assumed that their savings propensity is stable at 25 per cent, the answer is obviously £800. That indeed is

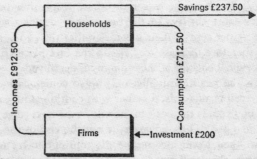

Figure 8

where the decline in income will be halted. Planned savings will be £200 and since they just match planned investment a new 'equilibrium' will have been established (Fig. 9).

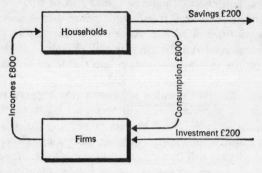

Figure 9

At this stage, until planned savings or investment happen to change again, the income level will remain stable. But it is 20 per cent below the original level – and it may be expected that employment will have fallen similarly. One Keynesian conclusion was to show that there is not a single unique equilibrium at the level of full employment, but that there are an infinite number of equilibria related to different savings and investment plans. The depressed conditions of the early 1930s, for example, were not merely a temporary deviation from a full employment norm, but the natural order of things in a totally unregulated economy. The possibility of the economy settling into a mass unemployment equilibrium stemmed from the fact that decisions about savings and decisions about investment were independent and uncoordinated. What brought them into line in the end was not the variation of a minor element like the rate of interest, but changes in the level of income itself.

The situation becomes still more complex if two further simplifying assumptions which we made at the outset are now dropped. We have been discussing the working of an economy without government economic activity and without foreign trade. Both, however, can be fairly easily integrated into the circular flow analysis.

Take foreign trade to begin with. If, when they receive their incomes, households choose to spend part of them on goods imported from abroad, it is foreign rather than domestic producers who benefit. Thus purchases of imports represent a further leakage from the circular flow. Exports, on the other hand, can be seen as an injection into the flow – an additional source of receipts to firms over and above those resulting from domestic sales. If the value of exports just happens to equal the value of imports, there will be no net effect on the level of domestic income. But if exports exceed imports, or imports exceed exports, the expansionary or depressing effects on the level of income will be similar to those caused by investment exceeding savings, or savings being greater than investment. So also with government. Taxes on the community are a leakage from the circular flow of income – they are no longer available for private consumption or investment purposes and are a destruction of purchasing power. Government expenditure, on the other hand, is an injection into the system, a further element in aggregate demand. Fig. 10 shows the place of these additional leakages and injections in the circular flow.

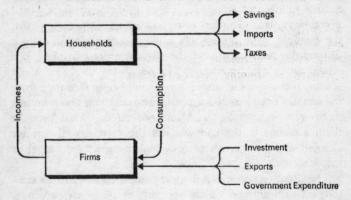

Figure 10

It can be seen from Fig. 10 that the condition necessary for maintaining any given level of income in the economy now needs restating. Instead of an equality between planned saving and planned investment, the condition now becomes:

Planned leakages (savings plus imports plus taxes)
must =
Planned injections (investment plus exports plus government expenditure).

So far as the private sector is concerned, there is no reason why savings plans should automatically match investment plans, or that import demand should equal export demand. Hence, if the government follows Gladstonian principles in balancing its budget (keeping expenditure in line with its income from taxes), the result will almost always be that the level of income in the economy is rising or falling.

It was the achievement of Keynes to show that a stable level of national income requires positive government intervention. Moreover, Keynes demonstrated that stability as such is not the appropriate target – for it can occur at any one of a number of income and employment levels. *Full employment*, far from being a natural outcome of the workings of an unrestricted market mechanism, can be achieved only by deliberate management of the economy in a way which was anathema to economists and politicians of his time. In Chapter 4, we will examine the policy implications of Keynesianism and their practical limitations when governments came to apply the techniques for managing the economy that he advocated.

4

Managing the Economy

Keynes was too late to tackle the problems of the inter-war years. By the time his ideas had gained acceptance and filtered through into official orthodoxy, Britain was at war again. In 1944, however, looking forward to the end of hostilities and determined to avoid the economic disasters which had followed the First World War, the government committed itself for the first time, in a historically important White Paper, to securing 'a high and stable level of employment'. The very fact that a government was prepared to take on this responsibility reflected a confidence that in principle Keynes had cracked the nut of mass unemployment, and that full employment could be attained by conscious manipulation of the economic system by the State. Moreover, an incidental byproduct of the more highly controlled wartime economy was that a mass of economic data – concerning national income, investment and consumption – had become available for the first time and could serve as the basis for managing the economy along Keynesian lines.

This chapter looks at Keynesianism as it was practised by successive post-war British governments in the period up to the mid-1970s. Present-day monetarist critics now derisively dismiss this as an episode illustrating only the harmful or irrelevant effects of government meddling. But in fact it can be argued that during these years the economy performed on the whole exceptionally well – a remarkable success story unmatched either before or since. On the other hand, there were certainly limitations to the effectiveness of Keynesian policies that became increasingly apparent over the years.

Principles of Demand Management

Keynes argued that an unregulated economy was extremely unlikely to hit on full employment, except temporarily and by chance. The reason for this is that the constituents of aggregate demand – consumption, investment and the foreign trade surplus – are determined by millions of largely independent decisions taken by individuals and firms in an uncoordinated fashion. The probability is that they will add up to a total demand either greater or less than that needed to purchase the output which would be produced at full employment. The sort of unemployment which Keynes was primarily concerned with (and there are others which we shall examine later) was that caused simply by demand-deficiency, a shortfall in spending by the private sector. Hence the equally simple solution – to increase total spending in the economy to the appropriate level.

In essence, the process of demand management of the economy boils down to two stages – diagnosis and action. The first task of the authorities is to form a view of the productive capability of the economy. If all resources were fully utilized, what would be the value of the resulting output of goods and services? Suppose that the answer which they give is £250,000m. Next they must inquire what the probable level of demand in the economy will be on the assumption that the government takes no further action. Suppose that their estimates suggest a situation like that illustrated in Fig. 11. Determining the total demand for the coming period involves looking at its components and forecasting the amounts of the various leakages and injections in the circular flow. In this particular case, the government starts from a position in which its budget is balanced, receipts from taxes equalling disbursements at £50,000m. The figure for private consumption, it has estimated, will be £100,000m. Exports are forecast as equalling imports at £25,000m., and savings and investment are also balanced at the same figure.

This is in fact a very simple case, with each of the leakages

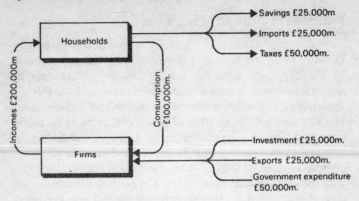

Figure 11

happening to match a corresponding injection. The economy is therefore in a position of equilibrium. The problem is that the total level of demand which is generated amounts to only £200,000m., £50,000m. short of the spending required to buy the output which would result from full employment of resources.

So much for diagnosis. What can the authorities do about it? If full employment is to be achieved, they must somehow fill the so-called 'deflationary gap' – and ensure that spending in fact turns out to be £250,000m. rather than the £200,000m. which will be spent if nothing is done.

Broadly, the government can adopt one of three approaches. Firstly, it can work on the private sector to revise its plans – take measures to stimulate consumption, investment and exports. Secondly, it may despair of the private sector and adjust its own spending plans to make good any deficiency in overall demand. And thirdly, it may hope that a certain amount of extra government spending will have a 'pump-priming' effect in inducing the private sector to follow suit. These three approaches are clearly not mutually exclusive.

Whatever its broad strategy, the government has at its disposal two major sets of techniques through which it can hope to bring about changes in the total level of spending – monetary policy and fiscal policy.

Monetary Policy

Keynesian monetary policy took two main forms: (i) influencing the structure of *interest rates* in the economy, and (ii) controlling the availability and use of particular types of credit – such as *bank advances* or *hire purchase*. (These must be distinguished from more recent monetarist emphasis on controlling the *total supply of money* in the economy – which we shall deal with in Chapters 5 and 6.)

Generally, monetary policy had a gentlemanly appeal to more right-wing governments because it appeared to operate anonymously through the market system and was administered at the grassroots level by the banking and credit institutions rather than by the government itself. That, at least, was the theory. In practice, the history of monetary policy over these years (and, for that matter, since) is largely one of a search by governments to evolve tighter techniques of control in face of equally persistent attempts to evade them by the financial sector.

Our concern here, however, is with the general effectiveness of such measures – aimed at influencing the consumption and investment components of aggregate demand. Neither, in practice, proved very responsive to interest-rate changes. Consumers seemed to take little note of the price or credit in deciding whether or not to buy, for example, new cars or other durables. And evidence shows that businesses, too, were relatively insensitive to the cost of borrowing when deciding whether to invest in new plant and machinery. Much more important were firms' views about the future prospect for the economy. If they were optimistic about coming expansion, they would go ahead with investment despite increased interest charges. If they were pessimistic, lower interest rates did little to improve their confidence.

Certainly, much larger and sharper changes in interest rates might have had more effect – but only by causing major revisions in business expectations. In other words, the danger was that while small interest-rate adjustments tended to be ignored, larger ones would be taken too seriously. As one commentator concluded, such policy was therefore either 'useless or vicious'.[1]

Nor did governments have much greater success with the other type of Keynesian monetary policy, control over credit like bank advances and hire purchase. Credit squeezes on the banks merely forced potential borrowers to seek funds elsewhere – from finance houses, insurance companies, extended trade credit and so on. Hire purchase controls, on the other hand, *were* effective in short-term demand management but their impact was a narrow one on consumer-good manufacturers like the car industry, which could then reasonably complain that their development was stunted by their being *used* as an instrument of government policy.

All in all, the history of monetary policy during the post-war years proved a disappointment to its devotees. Far from being an anonymous, non-selective and delicate instrument of control, it turned out to be blunt, harshly discriminative and difficult to administer effectively. Sometimes it failed to work at all, sometimes it succeeded by clumsy overkill and revealed a further defect – its irreversibility. As an element in the Keynesian battery of demand-management techniques it came to be relegated to a minor role, subordinate to the other major weapon of fiscal policy.

Fiscal Policy

For Keynesians, the government's ability to tax the community and to spend on its behalf gives it an important lever on the level of activity in the economy. Particular taxes and forms of spending can be adjusted to influence private consumption and investment. And there is also the impact on the economy of the total budget – how much the government spends in relation to how much it receives in taxation.

1. R. Opie, 'The Future of Monetary Policy', in *Unfashionable Economics*, ed. P. P. Streeten, Weidenfeld & Nicolson, 1970, p. 273.

In times of unemployment what, then, is the proper fiscal approach? First of all, to cut taxes on individuals and firms, in the hope of inducing them to increase their spending plans. In particular, the authorities should aim at redistributing income from those who tend to save a large proportion of their incomes in favour of those with a high propensity to consume. But there is more to it than that. After all, cutting taxes helps only those individuals and firms who are *paying* taxes. For those who aren't, an additional way of stimulating spending is for the government to hand out higher welfare benefits to households, and investment grants to firms for help in installing new plant and equipment. The government can itself also compensate for the failure of the private sector to generate sufficient purchasing power to absorb full employment output. It can expand the output of public enterprises and increase other types of spending under its direct control – for example, on constructing new roads, hospitals, schools and houses; it can build new factories and offer them to the private sector on favourable terms.

But who is to foot the bill? If the government is to spend more than it takes in from taxes, it will have to borrow or resort to the printing press to finance its deficit.

Such an approach might seem to be irresponsible in the extreme. To suggest that the appropriate policy is for governments consciously to encourage an abandonment of thrift, deliberately to get themselves into debt, appears to be the height of profligacy – a policy which might possibly have a short-term effect in stimulating demand but which is bound to lead to national bankruptcy in the long run.

Keynesians argue that the opposite is the nearer to the truth. Deficit financing stands a good chance of being *self*-financing. If it succeeds in getting the economy moving again, then output and income begin to rise. Even with unchanged tax *rates*, the tax *receipts* accruing to the government will automatically increase and be available, if so desired, for repaying the initial borrowings.

The role of taxation in 'functional finance' is a difficult one for the individual to understand. Most taxpayers see the purpose of taxation as simply to raise money for financing government spending. They may fear that some of it goes down the drain of governmental extravagance and waste. They may admit that much of it pays for a variety of useful services. But, in fact, this is only part of the story. For if we take the opposite situation to that of the 1930s or the present day and look at an economy in which total planned spending seems likely to exceed the value of full employment output, then part of the purpose of taxation is quite simply to destroy purchasing power. A government faced with an *inflationary* gap increases taxes – not to increase its own expenditure but to *stop* a certain amount of spending.

Very broadly, then, a government faced with excess demand should budget for a surplus; if there is not enough demand being generated, a deficit is called for. These were the fiscal principles according to which governments attempted to regulate the economy in the heyday of Keynesianism, with the budget being used as a major instrument for adjusting the amount of spending in the economy to the desired level.

The Trade Cycle

Active fiscal and monetary policy was considered necessary in the 1950s, 1960s and early 1970s as a result of the continued operation of what economists call the 'trade cycle' or 'business cycle'.

Periods of booming economic activity – with employment at a high level, substantial investment and general prosperity – have been regularly followed by recessions deteriorating into more long-drawn-out slumps, marked by rising unemployment and depressed business expectations. This, in turn, has given way after a time to a gradual recovery phase, leading ultimately to a further boom.

The causes of fluctuations are little understood by economists. The trade cycle is essentially a product of the uncoordinated leakages and injections into the circular flow which we have already discussed. But that discussion was in static terms – to show the nature of equilibrium and disequilibrium. The trade cycle is a dynamic process of demand and output incompatibilities being regularly repeated in a pattern of ups and downs.

Take, for example, an initial slump transformed by an increase in total demand caused by an injection of investment. This, we know, will cause an even greater increase in income (via the multiplier). In turn, this may result in a further rise in investment – if investment is responsive to changes in the level of demand. What we have, then, is a process of cumulative expansion, and it is easy to see that any downward movement in income will similarly feed on itself. Quite what causes the upper and lower turning-points of the cycle is not so easy to explain. Booms, for example, may come-to an end because of over-expansion of capacity or the existence of a full-employment ceiling or a revision of entrepreneurial expectations.

However, the fact is that fluctuations in economic activity between 1945 and the early 1970s were within much narrower limits than in previous periods. The trade cycle was still there but in a much dampened form – and, what is more, it was based on an upward growth trend. That is to say, each recession was generally at a higher level of real output than the previous one, and similarly each boom reached a higher peak than its predecessor. More recently (and since the abandonment of Keynesianism), the severity of the cycle has been renewed. Depressions have been marked by sharp falls in the level of economic activity. Unemployment has risen in depression years, without falling again in the 'boom' years of 1979 and 1983. Fig. 12 illustrates the continued existence of the trade cycle.

And yet from the end of the Second World War to the 1970s, with Keynesian techniques of demand management being used by successive governments of all political persuasions, unemployment was generally kept down to between 1 and 2 per cent of the workforce – almost incredible when it is compared with the inter-war average of some 14 per cent, and with the experience of the 1980s when unemployment has risen

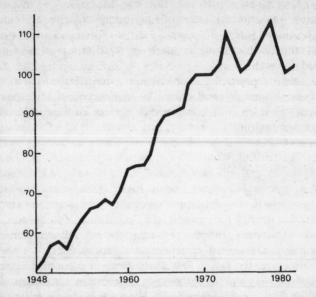

Figure 12 Industrial production. Base year 1975 = 100

once again to massive proportions. At the same time, the economy was growing faster than in any previous period – and prices generally rose by only a few percentage points a year.

It is not correct to attribute the success and buoyancy of the economy during this period solely to the use of Keynesian demand-management techniques. The conjunction of large-scale government spending on defence and social services, the massive increase in foreign trade which followed on the gradual liberalization of the international trading system, and a rapid rate of technological progress must all have helped to stimulate economic activity and keep up employment.

Nevertheless, *one* of the reasons for near-full employment must have been that governments put it high on their list of policy priorities to an extent which was only understandable from a Keynesian view of the nature and causes of unemployment. In the absence of the Keynesian breakthrough, governments might have resorted to deflationary policies (to cure, for example, balance of payments deficits) even more than they did. It is on this basis that Professor R. C. O. Matthews concludes: 'In this way the tendency for demand to be high for reasons independent of government action would have been checked by government action. That this was not done is something for which economists and the Keynesian revolution can take some credit.'[2]

The Barber Boom: a Case Study

The last British government wholeheartedly to espouse Keynesian demand-management techniques was the Conservative administration under Edward Heath. It was elected in 1970, actually on a platform of *reduced* government intervention and improved public-sector efficiency, and in October of that year published a White Paper[3] giving details of reductions in projected public expenditure. Its first budget in March 1971 was broadly neutral, although it made a variety of adjustments in tax rates. However, the economic situation then deteriorated, threatening to push the unemployment figure above the one million mark for the first time in thirty years. The Chancellor, Mr Barber, made the classic Keynesian response. In November 1971 plans were announced to speed up the public expenditure programme by bringing forward selective items of capital spending, and in his March 1972 budget taxes were slashed by some £1,000m. in the hope that industry would expand and take advantage of the resulting rise in consumer spending. By the beginning of 1973 the 'Barber Boom', as it has come to be called, was well under way. By the end of 1973 unemployment had fallen to 500,000. Between the first quarter of 1971, and the last quarter of 1973, real gross domestic output had risen no less than 10 per cent.

2. R. C. O. Matthews, 'Why has Britain had Full Employment since the War?', *Economic Journal*, September 1968, p. 569.

3. New Policies for Public Spending, Cmnd 4515/1970.

Here surely is a vindication of the power of Keynesianism – fast economic growth and a virtual halving of the unemployment rate in a matter of only two years. And yet the last decade has more frequently seen governments attempting to reduce unemployment by *cutting* public spending. Why have Keynesian techniques, used with so much apparent success for thirty years in post-war Britain, been abandoned? The main reasons for this volte-face will be explained in subsequent chapters. But for now we look at the *limitations* of demand management which became evident even to avowed Keynesians during the period 1945–75 and which will have to be tackled if their policies are to be applied again in the future.

The Limits of Keynes

When Keynes wrote his *General Theory*, the British economy was in the throes of depression. In the 1930s, *the* major economic problem was that of mass unemployment. Prices at the time were actually falling. Expanding demand, in Keynes's view, could only improve the economic situation. However, Keynesian theory came subsequently to be applied to a post-war economy with rising prices and buoyant employment. It is perhaps not surprising that, in these changed economic circumstances, Keynesian demand-management techniques should not have worked quite as Keynes foresaw. Three basic weaknesses of the Keynesian approach have become evident.

(i) There are the crudities of the fiscal and monetary techniques themselves, and of the economic forecasting on the basis of which they are used.

The ideal instrument for managing the level of demand in the economy should have four main qualities. First, we need to know the *direction* in which it will work – that pulling one lever will have an expansionary effect, while pulling another will dampen the economy down. Second, the *amount* of change must be predictable; the Keynesian 'multiplier' needs to be known so that we can be sure that the effect of policy on total demand is neither too great nor too small. Third, *timing* is also vital; exactly when is the policy impact going to take place? And finally, the ideal instrument of control would be capable of working in both directions and be rapidly reversible.

Clearly, Keynesian monetary and fiscal policies in practice fell very short of these ideal criteria. By and large, the direction in which they were likely to work *was* predictable but not their precise outcome and the time-lags involved. Such uncertainties were mainly the result of trying to manage demand in a mixed economy where two of its major components – private investment and exports minus imports – were inherently hidden from the authorities. The one depends so greatly on the *mood* of investors, and the other on largely external factors. It was also shown time and again that it is one thing to get a policy working in the right direction to begin with, and quite another to reverse it when appropriate. It is by no means easy, when the time comes, to restore deflationary expectations to their former optimism.

To make matters worse, governments were far from sure about what they were aiming at – or even where they were starting from. A mass of economic data was certainly available to them, but much of it was either already out of date by the time it had been processed or subject to substantial margins of error. Predicting the future from such data is a hazardous business indeed.

For instance, in 1972, the Government predicted that G.D.P. would rise 5·5 per cent. In fact, it rose only 3·1 per cent, an error of 2·4 per cent. In 1974, the Government projection was for growth in G.D.P. of 2·6 per cent. In fact, it fell by 1·1 per cent. And for all the increasing sophistication of economic models and improvements in data-gathering techniques, there seems little evidence that forecasts are any more accurate today than they were ten years ago.[4]

Using only the very broad Keynesian instruments of management, we are therefore unlikely ever to achieve accurate stabilization of the economy. The techniques, given the intrinsic

4. See for instance 'Forecasting in the Treasury', Economic Progress Report, June 1981.

difficulties of economic forecasting in a mixed economy, are far too clumsy to do the job effectively.

(ii) Not all unemployment is cyclical – that is, not all unemployment is caused by *demand* deficiency. Indeed, over the period 1945 to 1975, the most serious type of unemployment facing the British economy was not cyclical unemployment but structural unemployment. Cyclical unemployment, it will be recalled, is that where workers are jobless, not because there is inadequate capital equipment for them to combine with, but simply because the overall level of spending in the economy is not enough to buy the output which could be produced. Structural unemployment occurs where not only are workers jobless but where there is also no spare capital equipment available for them to use.

Structural unemployment in the post-war period has had a strong regional bias. Outside the South-East and the Midlands, unemployment has always typically been higher than the national average, as can be seen from Table 2. In regions such as Wales and Northern Ireland, there has been insufficient investment to provide workplaces for all those wishing to be employed.

Table 2: Unemployment (registered) percentage

	1968	1971	1974	1977	1982
U.K.	2·5	3·7	2·7	6·3	13·8
North	4·7	5·9	4·4	7·8	17·6
Yorkshire and Humberside	2·6	4·0	2·6	5·4	14·6
East Midlands	1·9	3·1	2·2	4·8	12·1
East Anglia	2·0	3·1	2·0	5·0	11·2
South-East	1·6	2·0	1·6	4·2	10·4
South-West	2·5	3·4	2·6	6·5	11·8
West Midlands	2·2	4·0	2·1	5·4	16·6
North-West	2·5	4·1	3·3	6·9	16·6
Wales	4·0	4·7	3·7	7·5	17·4
Scotland	3·8	6·0	3·9	7·7	15·8
Northern Ireland	7·2	8·0	5·5	11·4	21·7

Source: *Department of Employment Gazette*

The genesis of the regional problem – which has been with us for a long time – lies essentially in the loosening of ties which traditionally dictated the location of various industries. No longer do industries need to be sited beside fast-moving rivers or on the coalfields; the development of modern sources of power has greatly widened their possible choices of location. Nor is proximity to the source of raw materials a vital consideration for the majority of firms.

In these circumstances, locational pulls tend to be towards the *market*, with firms establishing themselves in areas combining a high level of prosperity with population density. Additionally, liberation from traditional locational influences means that the existence of 'external economies' now plays an increasingly important part in deciding where a new plant should be sited.

External economies are the benefits which the individual firm derives from working near a group of other successful firms. To choose such an area means, for example, that workers will be available who are used to working in that particular industry, and that the training facilities in the area such as those provided in the local technical colleges will be geared to the industry's needs. The transport and communications network, power services, housing and other social amenities will all tend to reflect the requirements of the industrial complex and the general prosperity of the area. The existence of a basic industrial concentration will attract ancillary firms, firms which use what would otherwise be waste products as the raw material for their own production, firms which produce components for the main industries. And, finally, working near enterprises in a similar line of business enables a firm to keep in touch with what is going on – to be aware of technical changes, new markets, new products.

The net result has been the gradual concentration of economic prosperity and new employment in the South of England. Even the West Midlands, the prosperous manufacturing heartland of Britain in the 1950s and 1960s, has seen its industries decimated in the late 1970s and early 1980s without any prospect of those lost workplaces being replaced.

Governments, recognizing that extra demand would not in itself solve the problem, devised a series of policy weapons to redress this regional imbalance. But the results of fifty years of such policy have proved disappointing and the regional problem is still with us, although it is now masked by the wider malaise of the whole economy. Reasons for the failure of regional policy include: over-emphasis on attracting capital-intensive manufacturing industry to the depressed regions, instead of labour-intensive activities; a failure to provide sufficient funds for retraining the workforce; and the frequency of change in government policy, which has induced uncertainty among businessmen thinking of investing in problem areas.

The relative unattractiveness of many regions was the main source of structural unemployment for most of the post-war era. However, the problem is now becoming a wider one – structural unemployment arising from the application of new technology. The micro-chip and bio-technology are just two of the innovative breakthroughs which are likely radically to transform what is produced and how it is produced. By and large, technical progress is to be welcomed because it reduces the necessity of hard physical work and the drudgery of labour. It also brings on to the market goods and services which consumers find highly desirable. More output from less effort also offers the possibility of increased leisure. But, at present, the benefits of such technology are unevenly spread among the community. Those at work are able to enjoy rising living standards and a glittering array of new consumer products to buy in the shops. On the other hand, the attractions of the coming technological revolution are not obvious to those denied the opportunity to work as a result of more automated production techniques.

From our present point of view, the important factor is that regional and technological unemployment can only be dealt with by 'supply-side' measures aimed at matching the necessary quantities of capital with appropriate labour skills. This will not be achieved by traditional Keynesian demand-management techniques: simply pumping more demand into the economy is more likely to spill over into increased imports rather than rising home investments. We shall return to this problem in Chapter 14.

(iii) Keynes was naturally concerned to a large extent with a single problem – that of finding a cure for the mass unemployment which was the plague of his times. Since the war, however, fortified by the increased understanding which Keynes brought about, we have become a great deal more ambitious. Governments have generally aimed at a *complex* of economic objectives; stabilization not only of a high employment level but also of prices and the balance of payments – all in a context of rapid economic growth. What has been shown during these years is that they cannot all be simultaneously and consistently achieved by exclusive reliance on the broad macro-economic measures of the Keynesian package. Given the imprecision of those techniques, all sorts of policy conflicts can emerge. Full employment, for example, requires that the 'deflationary gap' be filled by further injections of demand. But suppose that too much demand is inadvertently pumped in? Then spending will be greater than that needed to purchase output at current prices, and prices may be pulled up in a demand-inflationary situation. Getting rid of the bulk of mass unemployment through Keynesian methods requires only their crude application. Balancing on the tightrope between less than full employment and excess demand is a very much more tasking exercise.

The balance of payments too has acted as a major constraint on the use of Keynesian techniques. Thus expansion of demand in order to lower unemployment has often led to a faster expansion of imports than exports, with a consequent deterioration of the balance of payments – to which governments have traditionally responded by cutting back on raising taxes, or by raising interest rates. For example, in the 'Barber Boom', the balance of payments current account deteriorated from a surplus of £1,124m. in 1971, to a deficit of £3,273m. in 1974. Admittedly, part of the deterioration was caused by the spectacular increase in world commodity prices over the period, but a large part can be attributed to the high economic growth of the time.

The failure of post-war governments to achieve all of their objectives simultaneously led to what became known as the 'stop–go' cycle. Governments would react to rising unemployment and sluggish growth by implementing expansionary demand-management policies. Within from twelve to eighteen months unemployment would start to fall as the economy picked up. This was the 'go' phase of the cycle. But the balance of payments would then deteriorate as more was spent on imported goods and inflation started to rise. In order to counter this, the government would put on the brakes by applying restrictive fiscal and monetary measures. The current account on the balance of payments would improve and inflation would moderate. This was the 'stop' phase of the cycle as the rate of growth of economic activity slowed down and unemployment began to rise.

Governments increasingly felt trapped by these limitations of demand-management techniques and questioned whether Keynesianism *could* produce high growth, low unemployment, low inflation and a satisfactory balance of payments all at the same time. By the mid-1970s, indeed, the problem had become one of 'stagflation' – a combination of high inflation, rising unemployment and no growth. Many economists and politicians underwent a profound conversion. First, they came to believe that low inflation, not low unemployment, should be the prime objective of government policy. And, second, they rejected Keynesianism in favour of another economic philosophy – monetarism. It is to these matters which we now turn.

5

The Road to Monetarism

The first two or three decades of the post-war period saw a remarkable consensus between the major political parties on the main objectives of economic policy and the means by which they were to be achieved. Keynesianism reigned supreme and seemed by and large to work. As we have seen, the economic performance of those years can in many ways be regarded as an astonishing success story in view of what had gone before. And throughout the period, the primacy of full employment in the list of economic priorities was seldom questioned and remained an unshakeable commitment for all governments which, apart from anything else, would have regarded its abandonment as a sure recipe for electoral suicide.

However, by the mid-1960s inflation was beginning to rise more rapidly than before and governments, instead of just worrying about the trade-offs between employment, the balance of payments and economic growth, were forced to contend with this fourth major economic problem. Increasing emphasis was placed on the need to contain rising prices. By the mid-1970s many politicians were arguing that the most pressing economic priority was not to maintain the 'high and stable level of employment' promised in the 1944 White Paper but to halt galloping inflation. This turn-round in economic objectives was completed with the election in 1979 of a Conservative government whose paramount priority was to squeeze inflation out of the system at all costs – one of which might be substantially higher unemployment.

To understand this shift in policy priorities we need to examine the post-war economic record on inflation. Between

1953 and 1968, the annual rate of inflation was always under 5 per cent. It ranged from a low of 0·6 per cent in 1959 to a peak of 4·8 per cent in 1965. This was regarded as unacceptably high and led to the introduction of a prices and incomes policy in 1966. For a time, this seemed to work, but the late 1960s and early 1970s saw prices again rapidly increasing. By 1971, the annual rate of inflation had risen to 9·4 per cent. Another prices and incomes policy under the Heath Government was temporarily effective, but the remorseless upward climb in the rate of price increases had been resumed by 1973. By 1975, annual inflation had exploded to a staggering 24·2 per cent. The response of the Wilson–Callaghan government was a package of spending cuts, monetary controls and the so-called 'social contract'. Inflation dropped back to 8·3 per cent in 1978 but by 1980 was again up to 18 per cent.

Why Worry About Inflation?

High inflation might be regarded as worrying for many reasons. In the first place, it can cause an erosion in living standards if rising prices mean that we are able to buy less goods and services than before. However, what matters for individuals is not just the prices which they have to pay in the shops, but also how much money they have to spend. If prices rise by 10 per cent but we all have increases in take-home pay of the same proportion, then we are no better or worse off than before. What concerns us is *real* income – how much our money incomes can buy. For most of the post-war period, incomes in fact rose faster than prices. For example, between 1960 and 1970 retail prices rose some 45 per cent but incomes meanwhile doubled. The *cost* of living increased, but the *standard* of living increased even more. But, the opposite has been true of many years in the seventies and eighties; with incomes lagging behind prices, real spending power actually declined.

Inflation is particularly disturbing, too, when it shows signs of getting out of hand and becoming cumulatively worse. If workers and firms start building into their wage claims and price increases expectations of faster inflation, this will prove self-justifying because it will inevitably result in just what they feared. This is the recipe for 'runaway' or 'hyper-inflation' which occurs when prices rise at a faster and faster rate until in the end confidence in the value of money is totally destroyed.

A further problem caused by inflation is its effects on the distributive share-out of national income. It does not affect us all equally. The incomes of firms and shareholders, for example, are fairly closely tied to the price level; management are broadly in a position to fix their own salaries, ensuring that they keep up with current price increases; for many professional people and white-collar workers annual seniority increments provide an immediate cushion against price rises; highly organized workers have the bargaining strength to prevent *their* real incomes from being eroded by inflation. The real burden of inflation falls on those whose incomes are relatively fixed – either because of their weak bargaining position or because they are particularly susceptible to administrative restraint. Their ranks may include creditors and rentiers, but it is also the low-paid, some pensioners, and public-sector employees who are commonly hardest hit. Their lot is made even worse if the prices of basic essentials like food, fuel and housing are among the fastest rising – because low-income groups spend a larger proportion of their incomes on such items than those who are better-off. So the redistributive effects of inflation can be unfortunately arbitrary.

Also to be taken into account is the impact which inflation has on *savings*. The result of rising prices is obviously to reduce their real value. For example, £100 set aside in 1973 bought only approximately a quarter as much in 1983 as it did ten years previously. While inflation remained at the level of a few percentage points a year, this erosion of the value of savings was generally offset by the interest which they earned. But at many times during the seventies and eighties the rate of inflation has greatly exceeded the rate of interest. In such circumstances, it is possible for the incentive to save to be destroyed.

However, this is not generally what has so far happened. On the contrary, high inflation rates have often led to an increase in personal savings – as, presumably, individuals have tried to maintain their savings at certain real levels. Again, some of the weaker members of the community, like pensioners, have fared much better than average during years of rapid inflation because governments have gone out of their way to protect and even enhance their living standards. In particular, 'indexation' (for instance, the linking of interest rates to rises in the cost of living) has done something to offset some of the deleterious side-effects of inflation which have been mentioned. Provided that adequate attention is given to these matters and that real living standards are at least maintained, it might seem that all we need worry about is stabilizing the *rate* at which prices increase. In other words, we could learn to live with any given rate of inflation.

But in the case of Britain, or any other nation much engaged in international trade, this is not sufficient. To maintain our international competitiveness, we also have to ensure that our prices are not rising substantially faster than those of countries trying to outsell us in the markets of the world. If British manufacturing prices get out of line, it becomes more difficult for us to sell exports, and easier for foreigners to penetrate British markets. This is what in fact happened during the mid-seventies, when Britain was markedly less successful than its major competitors in containing the initial explosion of prices and then in reducing inflation to manageable proportions.

What Causes Inflation?

As we explained in Chapter 1, economists have not been able to offer an agreed analysis of the causes of inflation. They have been divided on this question as much as they have on the issue of unemployment. However, the battleground itself has shifted over the past decade or so.

For much of the post-war period, the debate was centred on whether inflation was caused by 'demand-pull' or 'cost-push'. Both of these could be analysed within the broad framework of Keynesian thinking. More recently, however, there has been the resurrection of a third, quite different explanation of what makes prices rise – the 'monetarist' view that it is due to excessive expansion of the money supply. We shall look at each of these alternative approaches in turn.

Too Much Spending?

Keynes himself was mostly concerned about the situation in which spending plans fell short of the level needed to absorb full-capacity output. The consequent 'deflationary gap' was the source of the mass unemployment which was the greatest problem of his time. But the analysis can also be applied to the opposite situation – that in which the various plans to spend add up to a total in excess of the value of full employment output measured at current prices. This is the problem of the 'inflationary gap', with total demand in the economy exceeding total supply. When there is large-scale unemployment in the economy, the effect of demand exceeding supply is to bring idle resources into employment again. The temporary excess of demand over supply means that retailers run short of stocks and increase their orders to the manufacturers. Provided that they are working in a competitive market, the manufacturers' response is not to increase prices, but to take on more workers and expand output. The increased demand *can* soon be met by an increased supply of goods and services so that there is no *need* for prices to alter. But at full employment (or indeed as full employment is approached), any excess demand in the economy can only show itself in the form of higher prices. As we try to spend our increased incomes, since there are no more goods and services available, all that will happen is that the prices which we pay are pulled up by our increased expenditure.

Demand-pull inflation is a very likely condition in mixed

economies accepting a wide range of social responsibilities and practising Keynesian stabilization techniques. Partly it is a matter of trying to do too much. The government wants resources for its welfare programmes, for defence spending, for education and the rest. At the same time it is stimulating the private sector to undertake more investment to modernize and expand production. Consumers are constantly bidding to increase their material standards of living. These competing demands may easily exceed the output which can be produced from available resources. But how can they be trimmed down? Partly the problem is one of priorities – with governments reluctant to reduce this or that particularly pressing programme of expenditure; too much is finally left in, with the hope that the rate of economic growth will somehow prove sufficient to accommodate the lot. Partly it is a matter of not really knowing what, for example, private investment or exports are actually going to amount to.

Together, these difficulties mean that excess-demand inflation can be a real threat and it is probable that at many times during the post-war years it is this variety of inflation from which the British economy has primarily suffered.

The search for a solution led to the development of a body of economic thinking during the sixties reaching a conclusion which was distinctly prophetic, if unpalatable. Some economists argued that the real cure to demand inflation was the creation of more spare capacity in the economy. Since prices began to rise before full employment was reached and since, anyway, stabilization techniques were far too crude to keep the economy at just the full-employment level, the answer was to work with sufficient unemployment both to eliminate excess demand and to leave room for the possibility of 'overshooting'.

However, before considering the more detailed policy implication of this thesis, we should first look at a second Keynesian explanation of inflation – that which sees the pressure of costs as the main element in rising prices.

Costs and Prices

Cost-push theorists need not deny the possibility of excess-demand inflation. What they do argue is that, even when demand is quite evidently not excessive, inflation can still come about independently through pressures operating on the supply side. When firms' prices generally are composed of costs plus an appropriate mark-up for profits, rising costs will soon be reflected in rising prices regardless of the state of overall demand – as businesses struggle to maintain their profit margins.

This approach has been a popular explanation of the inflationary process. For which element in costs has risen most persistently and relentlessly over the years? The real culprit, it is argued, is exorbitant wage increases. When wage rates increase by over 16 per cent, as they did, for example, in 1980, need one look any further for the causes of current inflation? Here, then, is the spectre of organized labour so powerful as to hold the country to ransom. An academic pointer to the way in which wage-inflation might be dealt with came from the historical researches of Professor A. W. Phillips, which suggested that there had been a long-term relationship in the United Kingdom between the percentage of unemployment and the annual rate of wage-rate change.[1] The higher the percentage unemployed, the lower the rate at which wages increased. There was a clear 'trade-off' between employment and price stability, which meant that society would have to face up to a decidedly awkward choice about priorities (Fig. 13).

The Phillips curve was first found to hold good for the period 1861–1913. But, remarkably, further work showed that the relationship between unemployment and wage-rate changes remained fairly stable during the radically different conditions which prevailed during the inter-war years and the post-war period up to the mid-sixties. It looked very much as though

1. A. W. Phillips, 'The Relation between Unemployment and the Rate of Change of Money Wage Rates in the United Kingdom, 1861–1957', *Economica*, November 1958.

it could serve both as a predictive tool for forecasting future changes, and also as a basis on which painful policy decisions would have to be taken.

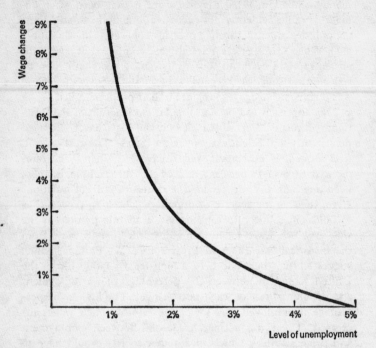

Figure 13. A Phillips curve

In this latter respect, the argument for running the economy with some excess capacity and the Phillips relationship both signposted the same course of action. Doubt about whether the country was suffering from demand-pull or cost-push inflation could be relegated to quarrelsome academics, because both sorts of inflation called for the same solution. If price stability was the main policy priority, it could be achieved only by modifying what had hitherto been regarded as the most sacrosanct of objectives – full employment. Deliberately created unemployment – only, it was argued, of relatively minor proportions – would kill both birds with one stone. On the one hand, it would strike directly at the roots of any excess demand in the economy. On the other, by reducing trade union militancy or whatever other causal process was hidden behind the Phillips curve, *cost*-inflation would at the same time be brought under control.

One of the great laments of those economists who aspire to be real scientists is their inability to manipulate economic forces in laboratory conditions in the way that their counterparts in physics and chemistry are able to do. But, as luck would have it, they were actually given the opportunity – in the late 1960s and early 1970s – to see an experiment. Unemployment, for reasons we have already discussed, *was* allowed by the government to increase. The Phillips hypothesis suggested that the result would be a dampening down of the rate of wage increases; and this, in turn, should have meant a reduction in the rate of inflation.

But it did not happen. As unemployment rose so also did wage rates; trade union militancy in bargaining for wage rises increased rather than diminished. And higher unemployment was accompanied by still faster inflation. The Phillips relationship had broken down.

The Monetarist Counter-revolution

The mid-1970s saw the beginnings of a sea-change in the nature and course of British economic policy. In the first place, inflation came to be seen as the major economic problem on which governments should concentrate their attention. Opinion polls of the time showed that achieving greater price stability had usurped unemployment as the economic issue of greatest public concern. Partly this was because *everybody* experienced the effects of inflation. Even those who benefited from it – perhaps because they belonged to a powerful trade union able to secure substantial wage increases, or because they had mortgages borrowed at rates of interest well below the rate of inflation – frequently still *felt* worse off. Pay increases came only once a year, but every day of the year they could see prices of familiar products going up in the shops. Unemployment, on the other hand, affected relatively few. For the majority, unemployment was something to be read about in the history books, with full employment since 1940 dulling memories of the 1930s.

In the second place there was a fundamental questioning about whether, after all, Keynesian techniques were relevant and effective in achieving our economic objectives. Controlling inflation, it was claimed, was not an alternative to high employment but the necessary condition for its attainment. Keynesianism, it was increasingly argued, was inherently inflationary: it had failed because its analysis of the causes of inflation and unemployment was wrong.

By September 1976 it was a Labour Prime Minister, Jim Callaghan, who in effect presided over the demise of Keynesianism when he told his party conference: 'We used to think you could spend your way out of a recession and increase employment by cutting taxes and boosting government spending. I tell you in all candour that the option no longer exists and that in so far as it did ever exist, it only worked by injecting inflation into the economy. And each time that happened, the average level of unemployment has risen. Higher inflation followed by higher unemployment. That is the history of the last twenty years.' With the election of the Thatcher government in 1979, the official rejection of Keynesianism was complete.

What has taken its place? Not, as might have been expected, some new grand design based on a fresh revolutionary breakthrough in economic thinking comparable to that which Keynes himself seemed to have achieved. Instead, curiously, there has been a reversion to just those 'habitual modes of thought and expression' from which Keynes had laboriously struggled to escape. Thus, with regard to inflation, we have witnessed a resurrection in the guise of 'new monetarism' of an economic theory which predated Keynes by at least two hundred years.

This 'Quantity Theory of Money', as it was earlier known,

stated a simple causal relationship between money and prices. For any given level of national output, the greater the amount of money in circulation, the higher would be the price level. If the volume of national output remained constant and the money supply was allowed to increase by 10 per cent, then inflation of a similar order was bound to result. The answer to inflation therefore lay in keeping the quantity of money under strict control. If the rate of economic growth was, say, 3 per cent per annum, then this should be the rate, too, at which the money supply should be expanded. Allowing the quantity of money to grow more rapidly than the volume of transactions which it had to finance would simply mean higher prices. The Keynesian revolution, with its emphasis on spending rather than money supply as the main strategic variable, seemed to have dealt the Quantity Theory a fatal blow.

But not all economists were so persuaded. In particular, a group of economists at the University of Chicago led by Milton Friedman were busy reformulating the traditional Quantity Theory of money on the basis of a series of statistical studies of the U.S. and other economies. Gradually, their work and that of monetarist disciples elsewhere built up into a formidable and influential counter-attack.

What their work appeared to show was that over a long period of time the correlation between money supply and the level of economic activity had, for industrial economies, been an extremely close one.[2] On the basis of this statistical relationship, the new monetarists argued that tightly disciplined control of the money supply stood a far better chance of achieving economic stabilization than all the 'meddling' of Keynesian techniques.

2. The most formidable evidence is contained in the massive study by Friedman and Anna Schwartz, *Monetary Trends in the United States and United Kingdom: their relation to Income, Prices and Interest Rates 1867–1975*. However, the statistical basis of this work has now been fundamentally questioned by Professor David F. Hendry and Neil R. Ericsson, who in effect accuse Friedman and Schwartz of quite unjustified manipulation of the figures to produce the answers for which they were looking; *Assertion without Empirical Evidence*, Bank of England, December 1983.

A case in point that illustrates the difference in the two approaches is that of the 'Barber Boom' of the early 1970s that we looked at earlier as the last full-blooded attempt at Keynesian expansion. As we saw, it had considerable success in raising output and reducing unemployment – but was accompanied by inflation rising to no less than 25 per cent by 1975. For demand-pull theorists, part of the rise in prices could be accounted for by an excessive injection of spending which was allowed to feed property speculation rather than be channelled into productive investment. For those emphasizing the cost-push element in inflation, it was the rise in import prices (particularly the quadrupling of oil prices between 1973 and 1974) that was the main villain of the piece.

But for monetarists an altogether different message came through loud and clear. Between the beginning of 1971 and the end of 1974, the money supply rose by no less than 92 per cent. Now, new monetarists argue that there is a time-lag between increases in the money supply and the resulting higher prices. So if there was a link between the money supply and inflation in the early 1970s, we would expect to see prices increasing in a later time period. And that is just what happened. Assuming a time-lag of one year, prices rose 77 per cent over the period from 1972 to 1975. Assuming a time-lag of two years, prices rose 84 per cent between 1973 and 1976. Whichever way one looks at the statistics it is indisputable that the early 1970s saw a massive increase in the money supply and that there was subsequently a massive increase in the rate of inflation.

Managing Money

Since 1976, governments have published 'targets' for the growth in the quantity of money. And by 1979, control over the money supply had become the key variable by which government aimed to regulate the economy.

However, for several years governments consistently failed to meet these targets and it was only by 1982–3 (with unemployment already over 3 million and with industrial output greatly reduced) that the growth of the money stock began to be held within the ranges set by the Chancellor.

This might seem rather strange, given that the government controls the Bank of England and the Royal Mint. Surely it is in a position where it can unequivocally decide the amount of money in circulation? Unfortunately, it is not so simple.

(i) There is the question of just what *is* this 'money supply' that is to be controlled? For most people, money is equated with notes and coins. What makes notes and coins money in our society is that people are prepared to exchange goods and services for these pieces of paper and metal. But in fact anything which is generally acceptable in payment of debts is money. Cigarettes performed this function in a defeated Germany in 1945. Pigs, shells, and wives have been used in other societies. However, notes and coins are now a relatively insignificant means of paying debts in our society. Cheques are far more important. A cheque itself is not money – it may bounce. But what *is* money is the balance in the current account on which the cheque is drawn. So, current account deposits have equal claim to be included in the money supply. But isn't a balance in a deposit account at a bank surely money too? After all, many banks today offer withdrawals on demand from such accounts (subject to a small interest penalty), or at most seven days' notice has to be given. And if bank deposit accounts are to be included, why not similar accounts in building societies and at the post office? What we have, in fact, is a wide spectrum of liquidity (immediate purchasing power) of financial assets ranging from notes and coin to, for example, stocks and shares. Attempts to define the money supply involve drawing a dividing line somewhere along this spectrum. On the one side of this line is 'money' and on the other 'non-money'. Yet on either side of the line the assets are very similar.

This ambivalence about just what constitutes money is reflected in the wide variety of official figures published by the Bank of England. These statistical series show the behaviour of totals of widening definition: M_0 (notes and coin) through a number of 'motorways' like M_1 (notes and coin plus current account deposits) and $\pounds M_3$ (including deposit accounts at banks) to the still more comprehensive PSL_2 (Public Sector Liquidity) which embraces building society deposits and the like.

For traditional Keynesians, the controversy concerning what is and what is not money is of relatively minor academic interest. But for a chancellor bent on regulating *the* money supply, the question of precisely what it is that he is trying to control becomes critical. In practice it was originally $\pounds M_3$ (sterling M_3) to which governments paid most attention (albeit with little practical success) although more recently they have resorted to keeping a looser watch on movements of *all* the possibly relevant totals.

(ii) Banks themselves create money, that is, bank deposits, by making loans. It was once thought that the Bank of England could, nonetheless, exercise control over their ability to do so by affecting the cash or liquidity bases on which they worked.

However, post-war experience even prior to the revival of monetarism showed the immense difficulties in making the financial sector behave as the authorities wished it to. Either the banks would find ways of circumventing official attempts at control – or new financial institutions would develop outside the ambit of such regulation. The traditional methods of monetary control – like open-market operations, special deposits, requests and even directives – will, if possible, be thwarted by the financial sector since they threaten its potential profits. An embarrassing example of this was revealed with the abolition of a particularly esoteric form of control, the Supplementary Special Deposits scheme (known in the trade as 'the corset') in June 1980. As a result, in a single month $\pounds M_3$ rose by no less than $\pounds 3,500m$. as money which had been put into channels outside the control of the Bank of England (and therefore not included in the $\pounds M_3$ statistics) returned to the conventional banking system.

(iii) Aware of these problems in controlling the supply of money, the authorities have, since 1979, largely concentrated instead on trying to regulate the *demand* for money in the hope that if that could be restrained then the banks and other financial institutions would have no inducement to increase its supply.

Now where does the demand for money come from? (It should be noted that by 'demand for money' we do not, of course, mean that we would all like to be richer by having more of it. It refers to the desire of households and enterprises to hold their wealth in the form of money *rather* than other assets.)

The demand for money stems from two main sources. First, the private sector – individuals and companies. And second, the government itself – as one of the means by which it finances its spending programmes.

Accordingly, since 1979 policy has broadly taken the form of a two-pronged attack. To reduce private sector demand for money, interest rates were pushed up to levels which were at times unprecedentedly high. And in addition, government has tried to reduce its own demand for money by cutting down the amount that it borrows. The details of this approach will be dealt with in the following chapter.

However, as we have already noted, such measures did not succeed in bringing the quantity of money within target levels, at least during the early years of the attempted monetarist experiment.

And yet between 1980 and 1983 the rate of inflation fell dramatically – *despite* failure to control the money supply. What *did* occur during these years was a massive downturn in the economy, with public-spending cuts, higher taxes and record interest rates combining to push the economy into a depression the likes of which had not been seen since the 1930s.

For monetarists, this might be seen as a necessary short-term side-effect – the price to be paid for reducing the rate of inflation. But for others, it was this deflation of economic activity rather than regulation of the money supply that had *caused* inflation to fall.

Perhaps Keynesianism can, after all, provide not only a better explanation of the decline in inflation in the early 1980s but also alternative policy solutions that would have obviated the need to throw millions more onto the dole queue. It is to the economics of recession, however, that we now turn our attention.

6

The Economics of Recession

British manufacturing industry is in a state of crisis. Almost every year between the end of the Second World War and 1973, output of manufacturing industry rose. The oil crisis of the mid-1970s resulted in a temporary fall in output, but by 1976 manufacturing output had resumed its upward march. Then, in the space of just four years, eleven years of industrial advance was completely wiped out. Between 1979 and the second quarter of 1983, manufacturing output fell by nearly 14 per cent: Britain's manufacturers were producing less than they were in 1968. If manufacturing industry was badly hit, then the corresponding figures for the construction industry were nothing short of catastrophic. Construction output was down to a level approximately equal to 1960. The index of industrial production covering mining and manufacturing, manufacturing, construction, and the gas, electricity and water industry declined by nearly 7 per cent between 1979 and the second quarter of 1983. We produced less in 1983 than in 1973. These figures were of more than academic interest to the 1·7 million people who were added to the dole queues between 1979 and 1983. It was their jobs that disappeared along with the lost production. In the West Midlands, the manufacturing heartland of Britain, unemployment rose from approximately 5 per cent in 1979 to 15 per cent in 1983.

What was the cause of the worst recession seen in Britain since the 1930s? There is no doubt that it was due to a complex of causes. In the first place, Britain's problems have to be set in the context of a *world* recession resulting from a failure to adjust to changing energy prices, the growing industrial potential of newly industrialized countries and the economic strategies pursued by the major industrial nations. What needs explaining, however, is why Britain, with its own oil and gas, has suffered relatively so much worse than others not so fortunately endowed. In the second place, it can be argued that Britain is undergoing a major technological revolution, with a consequent substitution of capital for labour causing reduced job opportunities; but this would seem more a threat for the future than an account of what has so far happened. And third, it can be claimed that a side-effect of North Sea oil has been to push Britain's foreign exchange rate to levels that have greatly encouraged imports and dampened exports, again resulting in lower domestic production. These three factors find their place elsewhere in this book. For now, we concentrate on looking at a fourth element contributing towards our recent economic plight – the impact of government policies designed to curb inflation and put the economy on a 'sound' footing.

The election of 1979 was the first since the war in which the winning party had in its programme explicitly rejected Keynesian policies as positively harmful to the British economy. In the late 1970s, Mrs Thatcher and her colleagues had become converted to monetarism – the belief that inflation is caused solely by excessive increases in the money supply. And in seeking the cause of such over-expansion, monetarists frequently point to *governments* as the main culprits – in more or less *printing* money to pay for their spending. To understand how this might be, we need to understand how government spending is financed.

Public Borrowing

Governments are responsible for providing a large number of goods and services, ranging from defence to medical care and from lighthouses to prisons. Governments allocate approximately 45 per cent of total output in the U.K. They finance this spending in two ways. Taxation and other receipts pay for the vast bulk of the expenditure. But the rest is financed from borrowing. The difference between government spending and taxation is known as the Public Sector Borrowing Requirement (P.S.B.R.). This can fluctuate by large amounts as shown in Fig. 14. In 1969–70, for instance, the P.S.B.R. was negative, i.e. government receipts exceeded public expenditure. By 1975–6 it had risen to 10 per cent of G.D.P. By 1982–3 the P.S.B.R. had fallen to less than 4 per cent of G.D.P.

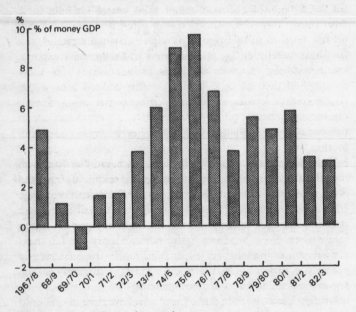

Figure 14. P.S.B.R 1967/8–1982/3
  (*Source: Economic Progress Report, September 1983*)

Governments may 'borrow' from two broad sources to finance a shortfall. One way is to persuade the private sector to lend them the funds. They can do this through a variety of schemes. To attract the small saver, governments issue Premium Bonds, National Savings Certificates and operate the National Savings Bank. For the larger saver, such as pension funds and insurance companies, they issue long-term government stocks. These are certificates which entitle owners to regular interest and their money back at the end of a specified period. Monetarists claim that the problem with this method of financing the P.S.B.R. is that it has consequences for the rate of interest. If government borrowing increases, so they argue, then governments have to compete for a larger share of a fixed pool of savings. The only way in which they can persuade savers to lend their money to them rather than somebody else is to increase the rate of interest that they offer. As a consequence, private borrowers who would have borrowed that money at a lower rate of interest are 'crowded out' of the financial market. Instead of the consumer borrowing money to buy a new car or a firm borrowing money to invest in new machinery, the government borrows the money to pay for its increased expenditure.

However, even monetarists agree that government borrowing of this kind has no effect on the money supply, and hence has no inflationary consequences. But it is still a source of concern for them in that it diverts scarce resources from the private sector to the public sector via higher interest rates. This is seen as bad for long-term growth. Part of the private spending which is crowded out would have been private-sector investment. Less private-sector investment means less new plant and machinery, and a lost opportunity to increase the productive capacity of the British economy. Ultimately, so the argument goes, that means lower growth.

In any case governments have an alternative to 'sound' financing of the P.S.B.R. Instead of genuinely borrowing the money they need, they can resort to the printing presses. From the time money was first invented, governments have found ways of creating extra money for their benefit. A popular way of increasing the total amount of money in a coin-based money system was to call in all existing coins, melt them down, add an amount of cheap metal, and reissue the coins. There was more money but the coinage had been 'debased'. In our modern economy, notes and coins form only a very small part of the money supply on any definition. It is bank money which dominates the totals. And today, governments have a perfectly legal way of creating *extra* bank deposits which they can use to finance their spending. They effectively do this by selling government stock to banks – receiving bank deposits in exchange which are then used to pay the nurses, civil servants, motorway construction companies, and so on, who receive their incomes from the government.

This, according to monetarists, is highly inflationary. The government has financed its excessive spending by creating new bank money. The greater the amount the government needs to borrow, the more it will be tempted to 'print' money in this way. This, to reiterate, is because it fears that an increase in genuine borrowing from the private sector will be associated with an increase in interest rates – not only politically unpopular, but also dampening the level of private-sector activity by reducing consumption and investment expenditures.

Keynesian fiscal policy – the use of budget deficits to alter the level of activity in the economy – is therefore seen as totally unsatisfactory by monetarists. Either it leads to inflation because the 'borrowed' money has been printed, or it leads to a fall in private-sector spending because money which the private sector would have borrowed has now been diverted into government hands.

The Conservative government of Mrs Thatcher therefore became committed to 'proper' financing of the P.S.B.R. and its gradual elimination in order to achieve low inflation, an expansion of private-sector activity and a reduction in the public sector.

Reducing the P.S.B.R. can be achieved either by raising taxes or by cutting public spending. Recent governments have strongly favoured the latter alternative. This is partly because of their belief that the burden on the British taxpayer is already too high – and that high taxes reduce incentives to work, both for workers and for entrepreneurs who own their own businesses. Lower taxes would increase effort and risk-taking in the economy, resulting in higher economic growth. Conservative governments have recently been committed anyway to a 'rolling-back of the public sector' on the grounds that it is the private sector that is the main source of wealth creation in the economy. Higher pensions and more teachers are all very well, but neither create marketable goods and services which can be sold in domestic and international markets. And industries now in public control would perform better when restored to private ownership.

So, for a variety of reasons, government since 1979 has argued that curbing inflation and increasing economic growth necessitates (i) the genuine financing of government borrowing; (ii) a reduction in the *level* of government borrowing; and (iii) a decline in government spending to allow room for a smaller P.S.B.R. and cuts in taxation.

In Keynesian terms, all this adds up to a recipe for economic disaster. Cutting the P.S.B.R. when the economy is at less than full employment, as it was in 1979, could only lead to recession. Indeed, as we know, it did. But monetarists themselves agree that although in the long run a lower growth in the money supply will reduce inflation, there will be a short-run transitional cost in terms of higher unemployment.

The exact mechanism by which this occurs is rather complicated – and debatable. Monetarists claim that households and firms have a clear idea of the appropriate relationship between their holdings of money and their level of spending – and that this relationship is a stable one. For example, if a household spending £9,000 a year thinks that a desirable money balance is £3,000, then its expenditure can be seen as 'turning over' that £3,000 three times a year. For the economy as a whole, the number of times that the money stock is turned over annually is known as the velocity of circulation of money, and it is a monetarist tenet that this will tend towards long-term stability.

So, if the government pursues a policy of restricting the growth of the money supply, households and firms end up holding less money than they would like, which is to say that their actual money balances are less than their desired money balances. To begin with, they may try to maintain spending by rebuilding their money holdings through disposing of other assets. For instance, they might withdraw deposits from building societies – but this and reductions in other financial assets will push up interest rates. But beyond this, they will attempt to restore their desired liquidity by reduced spending.

Both the disposal of financial assets and less spending lead to lower sales and fewer jobs. In the long run, however, when inflation is reduced below the rate of growth of the money supply, unemployment falls as households and firms now find that their money balances are *above* the desired level – and increase their spending accordingly. This is the monetarist argument. And according to them, the long-term 'natural' rate of unemployment at which the economy will settle depends on the willingness of workers to accept the wage cuts necessary to clear the labour market along the lines we described in Chapter 2.

What's Wrong with Monetarism?

So much for monetarist theory. Does it explain the workings of the British economy in the 1980s? On at least five grounds it must be strongly doubted.

(i) *Causality* As we saw in the last chapter, inflation fell between 1980 and 1983 *despite* erratic but relatively high increases in the growth of $£M_3$, the chosen monetary target. Indeed the evidence linking changes in the growth of the money supply and the rate of inflation is most unclear for any period of time chosen.[1] And even if it could be shown that increases in the money supply were associated with inflation, it would not necessarily follow that causality runs from money to prices.

To borrow Professor Kaldor's analogy,[2] every Christmas the British public sharply increases its spending. And every Christmas, if you look at the figures, you will find that the

---

1. See Hendry and Ericsson, op. cit., who find no evidence that the money supply 'creates either income growth or inflation'.

2. N. Kaldor, 'The New Monetarism', *Lloyds Bank Review*, July 1970.

amount of banknotes in circulation also substantially rises. Should we conclude from this that it is the expansion of the supply of banknotes which *causes* the increased spending by the public? It would be a very foolish conclusion to come to because the real facts of the matter are well known.

We spend more because Christmas, in our particular culture, happens to be a time of unparalleled extravagance and general benevolence. The note supply is deliberately increased by the authorities because our greater spending *requires* more notes to service it. It is not the larger note circulation which causes our wild spending at Christmas; it is the other way round. And each January, as spending by the public dies down again, the monetary authorities withdraw an appropriate quantity of notes from circulation.

Similarly, it is not perhaps surprising that the government's monetary targets only started to be met in 1982–3. By then, inflation had *already* fallen – together with output and employment – so that the money supply could be seen as simply adjusting to the now lower demand.

(ii) *Velocity*   There is a further lesson that can be drawn from Kaldor's analogy. Suppose that one year a Scrooge administration tried to curb our excesses by refusing to make the customary expansion in the December note supply. Would it succeed? Of course not. What would happen initially is that customers going to their banks to withdraw cash would be told by the banks, 'Sorry, we've temporarily run out. Please come back later.' However, traumatic incidents like this would not deter would-be spenders. Out would come their various credit cards. They would also find that, in the circumstances, the shops would be only too anxious to offer credit themselves. And meanwhile the banks would be doing their bit to ease the situation by urging traders to bank their takings several times a day. In other words, we should overcome the scarcity of banknotes by making the limited stock *work* harder, turn over more rapidly. In economists' parlance, limitation in the supply of money will be offset by an increase in its 'velocity of circulation'.

The financial flexibility of a modern economy is such that it is possible to accommodate pretty well *any* level of spending to a given money supply.[3] It even proved possible to overcome the extreme inconvenience caused by the Irish bank strike of 1970 when, for six months, the supply of banknotes and credit was completely cut off.

It is possible, therefore, that the observed stability of the velocity of circulation in the past has primarily been due to the fact that the money supply was allowed passively to grow in line with demand. But if monetarist prescriptions are now to be followed by governments there is no guarantee of its future stability since there are so many available ways round the attempted discipline.

(iii) *Spending Cuts*   In fact, despite the political rhetoric, *overall* government spending barely changed over the period between 1979 and 1983. All that happened was a change in its composition. Cuts in areas like education, housing and the civil service were largely offset by increases elsewhere – partly in defence and law and order, but mostly by a rise from 25 per cent in 1979–80 to 28·7 per cent in 1982–3 in the proportion of government spending on social security. In other words, instead of paying workers to produce real goods and services, it was now paying them to stay unemployed at home.

(iv) *Crowding out*   It is difficult to understand the notion of 'crowding out' in the British economy of the 1980s, with an abundance of 'scarce' resources lying idle. It makes sense to argue that if the economy is at full employment the decision by a government to build another hospital or employ an extra 10,000 teachers will result in resources being used up which would otherwise have been utilized by the private sector. But if the workers to build the hospital are currently on the dole queue, if the staff to man the hospital are ready and waiting to undertake training instead of being employed to clean graveyards, or paint churches on a government work scheme, then surely the private sector is not going to be deprived of resources.

3. Hendry and Ericsson, op. cit., suggest that even Friedman's own work reveals quite wide changes in the velocity of circulation.

And certainly the private sector over the period has shown no inclination to take up the resources 'released' by the public sector. Investment has declined, industry has lost confidence and firms are making plans on the assumption that demand for their products will remain depressed for the foreseeable future.

As to 'financial crowding out' through higher interest rates, three points need to be made. (a) It can occur if there is a *fixed* pool of funds available for division between the public and private sectors; but this is *only* the case if a government is pursuing a monetarist strategy of restricting the total supply of money. (b) To the extent that interest rates have remained high in real terms (i.e. they have fallen less than the rate of inflation), this is more owing to high levels set in the U.S. economy than excessive borrowing by the British government, which is to say that it is partly the U.S. economy rather than the British government that has been doing the crowding out. (c) Two other pressures on 'scarce' funds are the increased personal borrowing to finance the consumer boom of 1982–3 caused by the abolition of hire-purchase controls (mostly leading to higher imports), and massive privatization schemes diverting investment finance from new investment projects. It is not difficult to argue that it is the nature of the 'private sector borrowing requirement' rather than the size of the P.S.B.R. that presents the greater problem to be faced.

(v) *Unemployment*   Will increased unemployment prove to be 'transitional' as the monetarists predict, or have we lapsed to new levels of permanent unemployment? There is no clear evidence to suggest that the increased spending arising from the monetarists' argument about money balances will be sufficient to offset the more obvious deflationary consequences of applying their policies.

An Alternative Account

There is a persuasive Keynesian explanation of the recession of the early 1980s very different from that offered by monetarists. A government was elected to office in 1979, committed to cutting public spending, taxes, the P.S.B.R. and the rate of growth of the money supply. Trying to hold back the rise in the money supply, the government hoisted its own interest rate, the Minimum Lending Rate (M.L.R.), to a postwar record of 17 per cent in November 1979. The economy was already starting to move into recession in accordance with its 'natural' five-year cycle. The world economy was also moving into recession and exports were not helped by a rising pound which made our goods more expensive abroad. The result was a horrendous squeeze on industry. At a time when orders were beginning to fall off anyway, manufacturers found themselves in desperate financial straits trying to keep up with the much increased repayments on loans to the banks. They reacted in two ways. First, they borrowed more money from the banks in order to keep up with existing repayments – hence the rise in the money supply at the time. Second, they cut their costs as quickly as possible. Workers were made redundant or put on short time. Factories making temporary losses were permanently shut down, and firms de-stocked. Firms keep stocks of raw materials in order to maintain smooth production. They also may keep stocks of finished goods in order to satisfy orders quickly. Stocks are often financed through bank borrowing. One quick and easy way of realizing cash to cut bank borrowing was to reduce stocks of raw materials and satisfy new orders from existing stocks rather than carry on producing. Table 3 illustrates this clearly. Stock levels started to fall from the fourth quarter of 1979, and only started to rise again in the second quarter of 1982.

This reduction in demand for goods and services by firms was compounded by what was happening in the personal sector. First, the government found itself unable to cut public spending (mainly owing to the increase in unemployment), and could therefore only pursue its policy of cutting the P.S.B.R. by sacrificing its other policy objective of reducing taxes. The real burden of tax and national insurance contributions rose from 34 per cent of national output in 1978–9 to 40 per cent

Table 3: Value of physical increase in stocks and work in progress

	Quarter	£m. current prices
1979	3	1274
	4	132
1980	1	− 617
	2	394
	3	− 425
	4	− 2058
1981	1	− 1516
	2	− 1075
	3	7
	4	− 1576
1982	1	− 352
	2	− 492

Source: *Economic Trends*

in 1981–2. This inevitably cut disposable incomes and consequently cut consumption. Second, consumption was also temporarily reduced because of an extraordinary rise in the savings ratio. Faced with increasing inflation and fear of unemployment in 1979–80, households attempted to save more of their income. Between the second quarter of 1979 and the first quarter of 1980, the percentage saved from personal disposable income rose from 11·6 per cent to 16·8 per cent.

Keynesian theory argues that if consumers are reining back on their consumption and firms are reducing their orders for goods and services from other firms, then national income will decline. This is precisely what happened. The theory holds that unless aggregate demand is subsequently raised significantly, the economy will remain in its depressed state. That increase in aggregate demand is unlikely to come from industry. With the outlook so bleak, firms are reluctant to invest. True, firms did slightly rebuild their stocks from 1983 onwards but they were only rebuilt to cope with a reduced level of demand. The early 1980s perhaps saw once and for all a decline in stock levels. Increased demand is equally unlikely to come from a government committed to cutting public spending and reducing the P.S.B.R. Nor is the personal sector likely to pull the economy out of recession when squeezed by high unemploy-ment and rising raxes; as we have seen, the 1982–3 increase in consumer spending caused by abolition of hire-purchase controls (and a fall in the savings ratio) led mostly to increased imports rather than a response from the severely weakened U.K. manufacturing sector. On the international front, exports could increase, but again, it is unlikely that the increase would be significant enough to raise national income back to its full employment level.

According to Keynesians the recession of the early 1980s is a classic example of a contraction of aggregate demand leading to high unemployment. Nor, as Keynesians would predict, are there any signs that the economy will quickly return to full employment. What of inflation? Again, Keynesian economics can provide an explanation. The rise in inflation in 1979–80 was caused mainly by cost-push factors. In particular, the Iranian crisis in 1978, and the world economic recovery taking place at the time, allowed O.P.E.C. to push up the price of oil. While commodity prices rose, wages rose too as workers broke through the incomes policy which had existed since August 1975. The 'winter of discontent' in 1978–9, when workers from gravediggers to transport lorry drivers went on strike, heralded a pay explosion which was only to come to an end during 1979–80. Subsequently, as aggregate demand diminished, inflationary pressures in the economy declined too. Workers, finding their own livelihoods at stake, reduced their wage demands. Firms faced with emptying order books felt unable to raise prices even when faced with increased costs. No wonder inflation declined between 1980 and 1983.

Keynesian economics would suggest that government policies which aim to reduce the P.S.B.R. are perverse in such a situa-tion. Far from helping the economy to return to full employ-ment, they increase unemployment still further. Is the solution to our economic problems then to increase the P.S.B.R.? Un-fortunately, this 'naive' Keynesian answer may well be as damaging as cutting the P.S.B.R., if used on its own. British industry has been so decimated since 1979 that it is unlikely to be able to cope with an increase in demand. Instead, more money in the pockets of the consumer is likely to be spent on imported goods, creating an extra growth of jobs outside the U.K. As for inflation, those in work are likely to attempt to rebuild their real disposable incomes – reduced from 1978–9 levels – and to press for further increases as they grow accustomed to the now higher unemployment.

Keynesians of varying political persuasions argue that what is needed is a package of policies to cope with all these problems. British industry has to be encouraged to rebuild, with expanded demand a necessary condition – but one which might call for supplementary interventionist methods if required. Inflation must be checked by a further attempt at a prices and incomes policy commanding general support and understanding of its aims. Imports growth will need restraining – through devaluation or possibly even direct controls, if all else fails.

The road back to full employment cannot be an easy one. But for how long will we be prepared to persist with present policies before seeking a radical alternative?

7

Paying Our Way?

Between 1945 and the late 1970s, Britain was faced with recurrent balance of payments crises. For much of the period its international payments position seemed the most serious economic constraint faced by governments, forcing them into distasteful and painful policies and thwarting the achievement of their more cherished economic objectives. The balance of payments statistics, so remote from everyday life, must have appeared to the general public to embody their collective economic guilt, with the monthly publication of the trade figures reminding them of their national shame. Yet, looking back over the period with the benefit of hindsight, it can be argued that these difficulties, which seemed so severe and intractable at the time, were in fact relatively minor. Perhaps balance of payments problems loomed larger because other economic objectives – low unemployment and high growth, for instance – had broadly been achieved.

Today, economic circumstances have changed. On the face of it, the balance of payments seems to be no longer a cause for concern. Large surpluses on the current account, where our exports and imports are recorded, are notched up with great ease. But, as will be argued throughout this chapter, the balance of payments has in reality now become both a major cause and a symptom of our industrial decline. Precisely at the time when it commands least attention, it has become one of the most important economic indicators for the economy. Behind the seeming record of success lies a murkier story of industrial decay, loss of competitiveness and missed opportunities.

North Sea Oil

The nature and composition of Britain's accounts with the rest of the world have been dramatically altered with the advent of North Sea oil. Before, Britain commonly spent more on imports than was earned on exports. Take, for instance, the decade 1966–76 (Table 4). In only one year did the United Kingdom manage to export sufficient to pay for its imports from abroad. These figures refer only to the *visible trade account*. This consists of all recorded transactions between residents of this country and non-residents which involve the trade of merchandise.

Table 4: United Kingdom balance of trade 1966–76 (£m.)

	Imports	Exports	Balance
1966	5,384	5,276	− 108
1967	5,840	5,241	− 599
1968	7,145	6,433	− 712
1969	7,478	7,269	− 209
1970	8,184	8,150	− 34
1971	8,853	9,043	+ 190
1972	10,185	9,437	− 748
1973	14,523	11,937	− 2,586
1974	21,745	16,394	− 5,351
1975	22,663	19,330	− 3,333
1976	29,120	25,191	− 3,929

Source: *Economic Trends*

However, visible trade is only one part of our total foreign trade. About one-third of our trade is usually in 'invisibles'. These are current transactions which involve payments between residents and non-residents but in which there is no exchange of physical goods. Often these arise from provision of services of one kind or another – like shipping, civil aviation and tourism. If, for example, you spend your holiday in France travelling across the Channel on a French ferry, from the balance of payments viewpoint it is just as though you had imported goods from France into this country. A second important category of invisibles comprises interests, profits and dividend payments on past investments. Payments by Ford U.K. to its American shareholders represent an invisible import for the British economy (a payment from us to them); similarly, repatriated profits from subsidiaries of British firms abroad are invisible exports for us. In a third category there are payments arising from the activities of the government. Outgoings under this heading (U.K. invisible imports) chiefly take the form of maintaining embassies and similar establishments in other countries, military expenditure abroad and official aid to underdeveloped countries. Against them must be set the payments to U.K. residents which arise from similar activities of foreign governments in this country.

Adding the net balance of such invisible items to the balance of visible trade yields what is known as the *balance of payments on current account*. Since net invisibles have always been favourable (we have always earned more under this heading than we have paid out), the U.K. international performance looks a little more respectable when judged by the current account than when judged by visible trade alone. However, over the period 1966–76, although there were about the same number of surplus and deficit years, the total deficits on current account greatly exceeded the total surpluses. Since then, the situation seems to have improved markedly.

Table 5: United Kingdom balance of trade 1977–82 (£m.)

	Imports	Exports	Balance
1977	34,012	31,728	− 2,284
1978	36,605	35,063	− 1,542
1979	44,136	40,687	− 3,449
1980	46,211	47,396	+ 1,185
1981	48,108	50,976	+ 2,868
1982	53,316	55,548	+ 2,232

Table 5 shows that the balance of visible trade actually moved into surplus by the 1980s. The addition of net invisible earnings

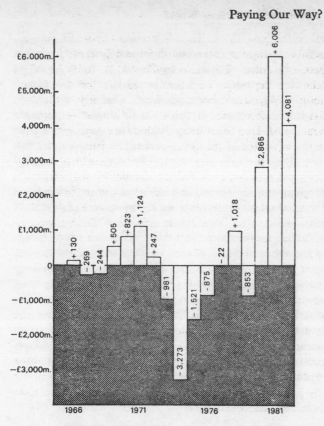

Figure 15. United Kingdom balance of payments on current account

led to the apparently very favourable position on the current account that can be seen in Fig. 15, over the period since 1976.

This improvement on the current account has been largely due to North Sea oil, which contributes to the balance of payments in two main ways. First, some North Sea oil is consumed in Britain, bringing savings on our import bill. Second, much of our oil is exported because it is a high-quality oil. Our refineries import lower-priced, lower-grade oil to mix with North Sea oil, leaving a surplus of high-priced, high-grade oil to be exported.

Before the mid-1970s, Britain produced virtually no oil. Therefore, as a rough rule of thumb, the benefit of North Sea oil production can be seen as equivalent to the value of oil exports plus the value of oil that would have been imported had North Sea oil not been exploited. This is less than the total value of production because Britain imports equipment and materials for the oil industry. Imports of oil rigs for instance represent a balance of payments cost to the British economy. So too do the interest, profits and dividends which are paid to foreigners who have invested or lent money for North Sea oil development. However, the total balance of payments costs of North Sea oil are far outweighed by the balance of payments benefits.

In Table 6 it can be seen that there has been a steady build-up in the value of North Sea oil on the current balance. But what the figures also show is that the non-oil balance is moving into massive deficit. The trade account of 1983 was historically significant in that Britain, one-time 'workshop of the world', imported more *manufactured* goods than it exported for the first time since the days of the industrial revolution. Its economic significance was that, without oil, Britain would not have earned sufficient to pay even for imports of vital food and materials.

Table 6: U.K. Balance of trade (£m.)

	Oil	Non-Oil
1980	+ 315	+ 870
1981	+ 3,112	− 244
1982	+ 4,605	− 2,373

In broad terms, North Sea oil has allowed us to consume more and produce less than would otherwise have been the case. It has allowed us to consume more because without North Sea oil foreigners would have forced us to correct our current account deficit. Just as with any household, if expenditure (imports) is greater than income (exports) borrowing or 'dissaving' has to take place. There is a limit to both of them. In a normal household, excess spending can be temporarily financed by drawing, for example, on building society deposits; beyond that, it is difficult to cash in money saved in a pension scheme, or even in an assurance policy. Similarly, spending over and above income can be covered for a while by running up debt with the bank, hire purchase or credit card companies. Fairly quickly, however, these will refuse further credit if there is no sign of the excessive spending abating.

The same is true with the balance of payments. Britain has 'reserves' of foreign currency that can be used to meet balance of payments deficits – but they are finite; and our large investments abroad are difficult if not impossible to realize at short notice in order to cover a shortfall on the balance of payments. Ultimately, if the situation is serious enough, recurring current account deficits need to be financed by borrowing from agencies such as the International Monetary Fund (I.M.F.). But if there is no sign that a national government is introducing policies to correct the current account deficit, then the I.M.F. may simply refuse to lend more money, plunging the economy into a state of crisis because foreigners will no longer be prepared to accept pounds in exchange for their goods – the equivalent of shops no longer being prepared to accept the cheques of a person who has run out of creditworthiness with a bank.

Correcting a continuous current account deficit would have involved Britain in either exporting more or importing less, or in some combination of both. Importing less would have meant that there were fewer goods and services available for us to consume. North Sea oil has allowed us to carry on buying imported goods despite the fact that we are not paying our way on the non-oil balance. North Sea oil has also allowed us to export less than we would otherwise need to have done. Instead of exporting manufactured goods for instance, we can now export oil.

Working less hard and consuming more sounds an ideal state of affairs. But for the British economy its consequences have been profound. Working less hard has meant that millions have become unemployed. Factory after factory has closed. The value of output has dramatically declined in some cases to levels not seen since the 1960s. The much greater volume of imports that we now consume at least partly represents goods and services which would otherwise have been produced in Britain. This is likely to be particularly true of manufactured goods – a sector which has seen a very sharp drop in output and a very sizeable turn-round in its balance of trade.

Looking again at Fig. 15, it can be seen that since 1980, Britain as a result of oil has been scoring large surpluses on the current account. And just as net saving is bound to take place in a private household, where income exceeds expenditure, so too with a nation: if Britain exports more than she imports, then either our reserves increase or the money earned will be invested abroad. We have argued that North Sea oil has allowed Britain to spend more and produce less. But for the fact that Britain has invested record amounts overseas since 1980, the increase in spending and reduction in production would have been even greater. It is this investment abroad that we now look at in more detail.

Salting Away the Benefits?

The current account on the balance of payments records the monetary value of international transactions, goods and services. If there is a surplus on the current account, then Britain must have invested, saved or repaid debt abroad. If there is a deficit, then Britain must have borrowed abroad, or sold domestic assets to foreigners. These are known as *capital* movements. There are a large number of such transactions made across the foreign exchanges, and the balance of the consequent outflows and the inflows must obviously correspond to the surplus or deficit on the current account. Examples of capital movements are foreigners (a) buying or building factories in Britain (direct investment), or (b) buying shares in British companies (portfolio investment), or (c) increasing their holdings or liquid assets in Britain (like bank balances) – to take advantage of higher interest rates, because they need them for trading purposes, or because they expect the value of the pound to rise vis-à-vis other currencies. These are all inflows of foreign currency. Against them must be set the outflow of foreign currency which arises from the corresponding efforts of British individuals, firms and government to increase their overseas assets.

As we have seen, North Sea oil has generated large surpluses on the current balance, and these have enabled corresponding investments to be made abroad. In 1979, the Conservative government made such overseas investment considerably easier by abolishing exchange controls. The exchange control mechanism, which had been in force throughout the post-war period, had forced British residents to apply to the Bank of England for permission to purchase foreign currency, with the Bank deliberately restricting the amount of money available for investment purposes abroad. This was a necessary policy instrument during a period when the current account was continually threatening to go into the red and when, therefore, it was necessary to try and stem the flow of money leaving the country on the capital account. North Sea oil seemed to make such a policy instrument redundant, because the current account was now so much stronger. The effect of the abolition of exchange controls was dramatic. In 1979, the year of the abolition of exchange controls, there was a net inflow of £2,307m. on investment and other capital transactions. By 1981, this had changed to a net outflow of £7,209m.

Using North Sea oil income for overseas investment has two main justifications. First, if it were not used for investment overseas, it could otherwise result in even more imports or fewer exports. The benefits of North Sea oil would be squandered on Japanese videos, and lengthening dole queues. Second, if North Sea oil is used for overseas investment, it will then generate foreign exchange earnings for us in future years. North Sea oil, instead of yielding benefits over just, say, the twenty years that it will last, will still be yielding interest, profits and dividends for our grandchildren. Investing North Sea oil money overseas is akin to the prudent pools winner who invests the proceeds and then lives off the resulting income.

All this is very true and soundly argued. But, there is a radical alternative to the two uses outlined above. Instead of using North Sea oil to allow us to buy more foreign consumer imports now or in the future, Britain could instead have deployed North Sea oil earnings to revitalize its declining manufacturing industry. For example, the surplus generated on the current account could have been used to purchase imports of foreign machinery and equipment – 'investment goods'. Instead of lending money to foreign companies to build up further their manufacturing base, Britain would have been investing in her own industry, with North Sea oil being used to create jobs in Britain rather than elsewhere. The large surpluses earned on current account could have been directed towards a major re-equipment programme.

Of course, it must be remembered that any surplus on current account is not earned by the British government itself but by companies and individuals exporting more than they have imported. What has been happening since 1980 is that other individuals, institutions and companies have then bought that foreign exchange surplus and used it to make investments abroad. To have diverted these funds into spending on imports of foreign investment goods could only have been achieved if the British government created a favourable economic climate, possibly with grants or tax incentives to firms behaving as they required – or with the government itself buying the imported investment goods for use in newly established state-owned enterprises.

The suggestion that North Sea surpluses should be used to buy foreign investment goods rather than being invested overseas, as at present, is illustrative of an alternative approach rather than a practical policy proposal. How much better anyway if British firms should produce as much as possible of the capital equipment needed to regenerate British industry, rather than import it!

In fact, North Sea oil made that feasible in a roundabout fashion. Had the government used its tax revenues from North

Sea oil to create an investment boom within a reflationary context, the foreign exchange earnings from oil could have cushioned any short-term adverse effects on the balance of payments.

In the past, the balance of payments has frequently placed a constraint on economic growth in Britain because whenever attempts have been made to increase the rate of growth, the current account has gone into deficit. This has meant governments having to deflate the economy in order to redress the deficit, and abandoning their growth targets. North Sea oil presented a unique opportunity for governments to reflate the economy *without* running into balance of payments constraints.

It would have been important to expand the economy in a way that maximized the long-term benefit from oil. Reflation through massive cuts in *personal* taxes, for instance, would have been unproductive since most of the money would then have been on consumer products, many of them imports. No extra investment need have taken place at all. What was needed was a reflationary package with a heavy emphasis on investment. Either public investment on railways, sewers, roads and hospitals or increased private-sector investment in response to tax inducements would not only have created employment in the short term but also enabled that employment to be maintained in the long term. And, for once, the balance of payments need not have been a constraint because of North Sea oil.

It was in such terms that the debate about the fruits of the North Sea was couched when the extent of the bonanza first became known. There was then general consensus that the benefits should not be frittered away and that the economy should be strengthened for the post-oil era.

In the event, as we have seen, the only positive contribution that oil has made is through *overseas* investment. The remainder has been squandered in maintaining imports at a level no longer justified by exports from a declining U.K. manufacturing sector. Ironically, the way in which North Sea oil has been managed has itself been a factor hastening that process of decline

– through the mechanism of the exchange rate to which we now turn.

Exchange Rates

What determines the rate at which one currency exchanges for others? Broadly, it depends on the strength of demand for it (the quantities being bought) in relation to the strength of supply (the quantities being sold). Thus the rate at which the pound exchanges against, for example, dollars depends on the supply and demand of pounds arising from dollar transactions coming onto the foreign exchange market where currencies are dealt in. Any sale of pounds (the supply coming from those who are buying dollars) tends to depress the price of pounds in terms of dollars. Demand, on the other hand, people buying pounds with dollars, pushes its price up. Fig. 16 illustrates these pushes and pulls on the exchange rate.

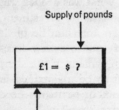

Supply of pounds

£1 = $?

Demand for pounds

Figure 16

The supply and demand of pounds on the foreign exchange market arise out of the various transactions which we have just been listing. U.K. residents will be coming to the market to buy dollars in order to pay Americans from whom they have bought visible or invisible imports; they will be *selling* pounds in exchange for dollars. Americans, on the other hand, will be buying pounds, with dollars, so that they can settle their accounts with U.K. residents who have exported to them.

Capital flows will have a similar effect. American investment in the U.K. will mean increased demand for pounds, British investment overseas greater sales of pounds. Fig. 17 shows how these various transactions fit into the picture.

Supply of pounds

U.K. imports
U.K. investment in U.S.A.
U.K. increase in dollar balances

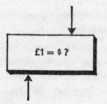

£1 = $?

Demand for pounds

U.K. exports
U.S.A. investment in U.K.
U.K. increase in sterling balances

Figure 17

If the supply of pounds exceeds the demand, the exchange rate will fall to bring the two into line – pounds will become cheaper in terms of dollars. Similarly, the rate at which pounds exchange for dollars will increase if the demand for pounds exceeds the supply of them. Only when the demand for pounds just equals the supply of pounds will the exchange rate remain constant.

North Sea oil has affected the exchange rate by influencing both the demand and supply of pounds. It increases the demand for pounds because foreigners need them to pay for the premium crude that is exported. The supply of pounds is diminished because British oil companies no longer need to import so much oil as before. More supply and less demand pushes the price of pounds upwards. This upward movement is likely to be

even greater because foreign exchange speculators will antici-
pate it, and buy up pounds to sell at a profit at a later date.
Thus between the last quarter of 1976 and the last quarter
of 1980, the pound rose from a low of an average $1·65 to
a high of an average $2·39. This was an appreciation of no
less than 45 per cent against the U.S. dollar. Over the same
period against the effective exchange rate for sterling – the
exchange rate measured against an average of other major
currencies – the pound rose 28 per cent.

This extraordinary rise in the exchange rate was not entirely
due to oil. By 1980, U.K. interest rates had been pushed up
to record levels in an attempt to regulate the growth of the
money supply. Consequently it became highly profitable for
foreigners to hold pounds rather than other currencies. And
finally, the monetarist emphasis on 'sound money' was one
which commended itself to foreign financiers who saw sterling
as a particularly safe depository for their surplus funds.

Government economists at the time argued that a high exchange rate was positively beneficial. It assisted in the attack
on inflation by keeping down the price of imports. And it encouraged producers for export markets (whose prices had been
made relatively unattractive) to increase their productivity in
order to remain competitive – or switch to 'up-market' products
where price considerations were not so important.

On balance, however, the high exchange rate was very
damaging to the British economy. In making exports dearer
and imports cheaper it combined with other deflationary
pressures in a tight squeeze on manufacturing industry. With
export orders difficult to come by and domestic buyers switch-
ing to cheap imports, closures and redundancies were inevitable.

Subsequently the exchange rate declined again so that by
1983 the pound was at the more realistic rate of $1·50, and
against other currencies had fallen to its 1976 level. This was
partly due to the upsurge of U.S. interest rates as President
Reagan embarked on a huge programme of defence spending,
and partly because of uncertainties about the future price of oil.

But by then the damage had been done. British industry had been seriously weakened. The 'strength of sterling', far from being a cause for national self-congratulation, had played a major part in that process.

International Competitiveness

We have just seen that there were those who argued that when the exchange rate was at its highest levels, firms would be forced into seeking alternative and beneficial ways of offsetting their decline in competitiveness by seeking productivity improvements and reductions in costs, and by moving up-market in their product range.

None of these arguments was even at the time very plausible or persuasive. Such was the *extent* of the competitive setback caused by the upward movement in the exchange rate that the required degree of compensatory increases in productivity was, for the majority of enterprises, totally beyond their capability.

What *did* result was a widespread 'shake-out' in British industry during the early 1980s as a consequence of which it is certainly now a good deal leaner than it was before. But is it also 'fitter'? Critics point to the fact that the recession has taken out both good firms and bad – primarily according to their cash flow and borrowing positions rather than whether they were inherently competitive or uncompetitive. What remains is therefore still a ragbag of efficient and inefficient – but less of them. There are now fewer firms exporting and fewer firms fighting foreign competition in home markets, with a reduced capacity to take advantage of any upturn in the economy.

Furthermore, the strategy of attempting to reduce real wages in order to become more internationally competitive is abortive to the extent that other leading industrial nations are pursuing similar policies. The international economy has always been an unordered jungle – as seen in today's battle of competitive deflation in the major economies rather than a concerted attempt between them to restore stability or expansion in the level of economic activity.

Is the Balance of Payments a Problem?

The balance of payments is a problem when our total receipts of foreign currency are too small or too unstable for us to undertake our desired level of foreign spending without recourse to unacceptable policies or abandoning other economic goals. It cannot be defined in any objective, technical, unequivocal way. It is all a matter of whether what is 'coming in' is sufficient (and of an acceptable form) to meet what it is the aim of economic policy to see 'going out' – and whether this can be achieved without forfeiting other policy goals. What constitutes 'balance of payments equilibrium' is a nationally subjective, highly political notion.

Thus, during the 1960s, for example, much was heard of Britain's balance of payments difficulties. But these arose not so much from a peculiarly British inability to export sufficiently as from the determination on the part of successive governments that the problem should be solved within a *given* political framework.

Thus it was felt right and proper that the U.K. should be a major overseas investor, maintain substantial defence postures in various parts of the world and offer considerable official aid to underdeveloped countries. All of these are clearly to a large degree *political* targets. Moreover, governments did all they could to achieve them within a context of *fixed*[1] exchange rates. The external value of the pound was held as near-sacrosanct by Conservative and Labour governments alike. Pri-

1. This was the system that the major economies practised throughout the postwar years up to 1972 whereby they held their exchange rates at certain 'par' levels to be changed only in exceptional circumstances and with the agreement of the I.M.F. They did this by intervening in foreign exchange markets, with the government itself selling pounds (buying foreign currencies) whenever the pound would otherwise have risen, or buying pounds (with funds from our foreign reserves) to prevent any possible fall. Since 1972, sterling and other major currencies have largely been allowed to 'float' and find their own market levels.

marily this attitude stemmed from a determination to maintain the role of sterling as an international currency – one not just used for domestic payments but one which foreigners, too, were prepared to hold as a means of settling their debts between themselves. It was argued that for sterling to be used in this way brought substantial economic benefits like the earnings of the City of London; but it was also seen as a source of political prestige – to put it bluntly, buying a seat at the conference table. However, given this use of sterling for international payments, the pound was in a highly exposed position. Recurrent balance of payments 'crises' could be all too easily manufactured. For as soon as foreigners, for whatever reason, thought that they could detect a weakness in the British position (or even a relative strength in other economies), they could switch funds out of the U.K. in a volume and at a speed which was quite alarming in relation to the British reserves which represented the major line of defence against such a speculative run on the pound.

If, then, there was a persistent balance of payments problem, it was a problem which to a large extent was of our own making. It was not international economics which somehow dictated that Britain should maintain extensive external commitments, encourage the use of sterling as an international currency and defend the pound at its existing rate. These were all policy aims on the part of successive governments – aims which other members of the international community were not always wholly sympathetic towards. Other countries could reasonably argue that it was time Britain cut its international political ambitions according to its cloth. This is in fact what happened. When the pound was finally devalued in 1967, there was a simultaneous reduction in Britain's external commitments – the withdrawal from east of Suez and restrictions placed on the outward flow of British investment capital.

Throughout this earlier period, the shortfall on the balance of payments was *marginal* and it seems extraordinary in retrospect that so many sacrifices were constantly called for to rectify so minor a problem.

Twenty years on, when today we hear relatively so little about it, the balance of payments is in reality a problem of a much more fundamental nature: (i) our increasing failure to earn sufficient foreign currency on the non-oil account to pay even for imports of basic foodstuffs and raw materials; (ii) the masking of this weakness by oil earnings that are now due to decline; and (iii) the fact that recent current account surpluses have been earned only with imports artificially reduced by mass unemployment.

The key question is therefore what would happen to the balance of payments should, for any reason, the level of economic activity in the U.K. recover and unemployment fall? It is a question that in particular has much exercised Keynesians who advocate a reflationary strategy in place of monetarism.

As we have seen, the problem is that certainly during the initial phases of reflation, imports will grow more rapidly than exports. There are those who argue that the brunt of this imbalance should be borne by a fall in the exchange rate. But this carries the danger, as such 'devaluationists' concede, that the consequent rise in import prices will trigger off a fresh wage-price inflationary spiral. Their proposals generally therefore also emphasize the need for an accompanying prices and incomes policy to contain such pressures – a policy that they claim it might be possible to introduce, despite past failures, as a quid pro quo for expansion.

Others are much more pessimistic and argue that the short-term competitive benefits of lowering the exchange rate will soon be cancelled out by consequent cost increases. Some, like the Cambridge Economic Policy Group (C.E.P.G.), have argued that the British economy is anyway now too weak to compete internationally and that recovery is possible only behind a protective wall of import controls. Just as the correct way to deal with a patient weak with fever is to protect him from excessive cold and feed him light food, so it is with British industry. The last thing to do with the patient is to send him for an early morning run with his German and Japanese competitors, both brimming with health. Import controls, on the other hand, will give British industry a breathing space in which to recover from the battering it has received from foreign competition. Relieved from such competition, British industry will be able to expand in domestic markets once occupied by imports (to be held at their present level). Industry will also feel far more certain about its ability to sell in domestic markets in the future. Higher present profits and expectations of higher future profits will encourage industry to invest. Investment will mean higher productivity, lower prices and better competitiveness. British consumers will be weaned off the imported goods for which they have shown such a liking in the post-war period. Having a firm domestic market base, and having invested heavily, British industry will then be in a much stronger position to compete internationally.

Critics of import controls can use one of many arguments. First, there is the real possibility that if Britain imposes import controls on foreign goods, then other countries will apply similar measures to our exports. Strong retaliation would eliminate any gains to be made from import controls. Second, import controls would raise domestic prices and reduce choice for consumers, at least in the short run. Third, there is no guarantee that British firms will use the breathing space afforded them to reinvest and re-equip. What may well happen is that they will simply put up their prices in the absence of foreign competition and distribute the resulting high profits to their shareholders. A lack of competition, it is argued, will considerably reduce the incentive for British industry to improve its goods and lower its prices.

But, argues the C.E.P.G., the issue is not really whether or not we should have import controls – but of what sort? Should they be open and explicit, or will they take the form of ever-increasing numbers out of work and therefore with reduced ability to buy imported goods and services?

Fig. 18 illustrates the nature of the problem. The straight lines indicate the growth of the economy that would have been necessary to maintain unemployment at various levels. The dotted line shows the increase in national output at which the current account of the balance of payments would actually balance. It can be seen that our recent trade performance has warranted a fall rather than a rise in national output – and still further unemployment.

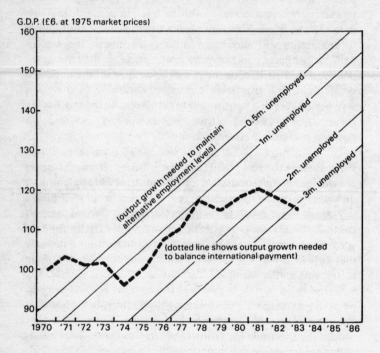

G.D.P. (£6. at 1975 market prices)

Figure 18 National output and employment
  (*Source: Simon and Coates*)

Can a vicious circle of low growth leading to balance of payments weakness constraining a move towards faster growth be converted into a virtuous circle of faster growth which improves competitiveness and eliminates the balance of payments as a constraint to recovery? Our limited understanding of the causes of economic growth itself is the subject of the next chapter.

8

Getting Richer

By 1956, a British government confidently committed itself in a White Paper to securing 'a rapid and sustained rate of economic growth'. Governments ever since have been desperately trying to fulfil that commitment. However, to think that rapid growth was even possible was a far cry from the pessimism of the pre-war stagnationist pundits who argued that mature economies such as Britain's had finally run out of steam and that there was little further scope for squeezing greater output from our limited resources.

That is not to say that there is anything new about the post-war interest in economic growth. On the contrary, it was just this problem – the dynamics of *developing* an economy – which was of prime concern to the founding fathers of modern economics in the eighteenth and early nineteenth centuries. It was this very matter – the 'causes of the wealth of nations' and how that wealth could be increased – which largely occupied Adam Smith and his immediate successors. Only in the latter part of the last century were economists diverted from this central aim into an examination of the minutiae of the economic system, the detailed rules for an optimum allocation of resources within a *given* boundary of production possibilities. And, of course, with the unemployment of the 1920s and 1930s, questions of expanding the economy's capacity to produce seemed quite irrelevant when even its current capacity couldn't be fully used.

These days, we have come to look back on the 1950s and the 1960s as some sort of golden age, when year after year national output increased. Yet then, as now, economists and politicians worried about why the British economy was not growing still faster. Then, as now, politicians were promising that their policies would be the answer to Britain's 'slow' growth. Today, despite continuous disappointments, the economic horizons of the mass of the people remain optimistic in this respect. Most of us would be surprised if our children did not live in an even more affluent society than our own. We are perhaps less sure that our own children will benefit from the affluence surrounding them because they may fall foul of the dole queue.

In this chapter we are largely concerned with the nature and causes of growth and will leave for later questions about how far economic growth can properly be regarded as an end of policy. To begin with, we should define what it is that we are talking about.

Thus, for example, if the total value of goods and services produced in Britain is £200,000m. and in a year's time it has risen to £220,000m., it appears that the capacity of the economy to produce output has gone up by 10 per cent. However, part of that rise may merely reflect inflation. If the prices of the goods and services which go to make up the gross national product have risen on average by, say, 7 per cent, the *real* increase in output (as opposed to its money value) is only 3 per cent. This is the growth rate for the economy – although, apart from eliminating the effects of changes in the general price level, we might also want to allow for population increase. If, for example, population has grown by 1 per cent over the course of the year, the growth rate per capita is reduced to only 2 per cent.

Confusion sometimes arises because there are two broad sources of increased output which are not always clearly distinguished. Firstly, production can be increased when the economy starts off with unemployment and idle capacity; this was the problem that Keynes was largely concerned with – how to ensure that an economy works at its full potential. And, secondly, increased output can be brought about if the potential itself is increased through greater efficiency in squeezing more goods and services out of our limited resources. It is the second of these, the 'growth of productive potential', which mostly interests us here. Measuring it involves comparing like with like, output in years when the margin of unused capacity in the economy is the same – say, 3 per cent. If, in another year, that margin is reduced to 2 per cent, clearly there will be an additional increment of output. But that will be in the nature of a once-and-for-all bonus – quite different from the effect of increasing the productive potential. In practice, politicians in particular are very happy to mix the two sources of increased output together in order to yield the highest possible overall growth rate for the economy.

Three further general points should be made at this stage. Firstly, growth measures the increase in output of all goods and services – it says nothing about *which* sorts of production have expanded, at what costs or who gets the benefit; it is a highly aggregative concept. Secondly, given the difficulties of measuring what makes up a national output of well over £200,000m. (and of deflating the total to allow for general price changes), it is not surprising that ostensibly precise statistical statements (for instance that the economy in the past year grew at 2·7 per cent) are in fact subject to a significant margin of error. Sometimes it is doubtful whether, for example, the economy grew very slightly or marginally slipped back. Finally, an initial warning that, although economic growth is commonly equated by politicians and others with 'economic progress' or an 'increase in the economic welfare of the community' or an 'improvement in the standard of living', it does not in fact necessarily indicate any of these.

First though, how well or badly has the British economy been performing in this respect? Certainly, there is a general feeling that failure to get the economy on a path of sustained expansion has been one of the many signs of a chronic British economic malaise. But is this view really justified? It depends on what is used as a yardstick for assessing the recent record.

To see Britain's post-war growth performance in the most favourable light, we should look backwards. Table 7 shows that, judged by what we achieved in the past, recent growth rates per capita looked decidedly commendable.

A growth rate of 2·7 per cent, the annual average for 1963–70,

Table 7: G.D.P. per capita. Annual % increase

1870–1913	1·6
1922–38	1·1
1950–57	1·7
1957–65	2·4
1963–70	2·7
1970–79	1·7

was a great improvement on what was managed at any other time during the previous century, including the industrial revolution, when Britain had a head start on other nations. And it should also be remembered that growth takes place at a *compound* rate: 2·7 per cent a year is enough to double the national output every quarter of a century.

Pessimists, on the other hand, should seek their comparisons elsewhere. That similar economies have fared very much better than the U.K. is shown in Table 8. Even if we set aside the impressive record of Japan, it is clear that countries much closer to home have all managed to achieve substantially higher rates of economic growth than we have. Depressingly, Britain is found to be propping up the international league table.

Table 8: Rates of growth, 1971–80

Country	Average per cent increase in G.D.P./head
Japan	3·7
France	2·9
Belgium	2·9
Germany	2·7
Canada	2·5
U.S.A.	2·0
U.K.	1·7

Source: *Social Trends*

Recent economic experience has proved even more disappointing. For instance, growth in national output over the decade from 1973 to 1982 averaged less than ½ per cent per annum. Between 1979 and 1982, growth rates were negative. The more optimistic of economic forecasts predict that Britain will be lucky to grow at 2 per cent per annum over the rest of the 1980s.

Why the British economy has grown slowly is a question to which a very large number of economists (and not just British) have devoted a good deal of their attention. As a result, there is no shortage of answers. Indeed there is an embarrassing number of them – the host of factors which have been put forward as relevant must grossly *over*-explain the problem. But, despite this wealth of analysis, the truthful answer to the question is that we simply don't know.

At an elementary level, it is possible to construct a model of the economy in which investment and savings are the key to faster growth. On this argument, growth depends on the rate at which capital can be accumulated. Suppose to begin with that the economy is producing an output of £100,000m. a year with a capital stock (of factories, machines, roads, mines, etc.) of £300,000m. In other words, for every three units of capital it has, it produces one unit of output (in economic jargon, the capital–output ratio is 3 : 1). If it is hoped that in the coming year output can be expanded by £5,000m. (i.e. a growth rate of 5 per cent on the initial G.D.P. of £100,000m.), then capital stock will have to be increased by three times that amount – new investment will have to be undertaken to the order of £15,000m. But where does this new investment come from? It requires resources which, in a fully employed economy, must be released from their alternative use in present consumption. The implication of getting the economy onto a higher long-term growth trend is that we shall have to make some short-term sacrifices. A larger national cake in the future means limiting our consumption of it today. Higher savings channelled into productive investment is the path to faster growth. The British economy has grown slowly because we have not been prepared to limit our demands on resources *now* in order to have more jam tomorrow.

Economists and economic commentators who hold this view

will point to the fact that investment in the British economy has been significantly lower than in West European countries. But comparisons of this kind are extremely difficult to make. Enormous problems arise in measuring everything that goes to make up the capital stock of a country. Should we concentrate on the figures for simply *net* investment (the addition to the total stock) or *gross* investment (new investment plus that needed to maintain the previous stock)? Numerous complications arise, particularly in the treatment of depreciation.

Putting to one side these purely technical problems, the fact is that anyway no very close correlation can be established between investment rates and economic growth in various countries. And, even if they could, the appropriate causal relationship would still have to be established. Would it be investment which was *causing* growth, or the growth of output which itself led to higher investment?

The answer is not known. What is obvious is that investment is very much a hold-all concept. Whether additions to the capital stock result in faster growth must depend on what sort of investment is being undertaken. The impact on output of building new hospitals, new office blocks or new factories is not likely to be the same. Again, the extent to which new capital is used effectively may be as important a consideration as the total itself. The age structure of the capital stock is also important; part of the post-war success of the continental countries may be attributable to the fact that they were unfortunate enough to suffer much greater wartime destruction of their capital assets than we did and consequently were forced to replace them by more efficient and up-to-date equipment.

What has become clear from the researches of those interested in the question of why growth rates between economies differ is that there are multiple influences to take into account. There is no single economic variable which can be manipulated to break through from a low to a faster rate of economic growth. Professor E. F. Denison, for example, in his mammoth study of *Why Growth Rates Differ*,[1] suggested no less than sixteen

1. Brookings Institution, Washington, 1967.

different relevant factors and tried to measure their relative significance. These included factors as diverse as the limited size of the British market, the mature industrial state of the occupational structure of the British population and poor management of the economy.

In the end, as someone has written, analyses of the causes of economic growth are inevitably reduced to exercises in 'amateur sociology'. Professor Denison's study concluded that the difference of growth rates between various countries could be only partially explained in terms of quantifiable economic factors. There remained a substantial 'residual element' which still had to be accounted for. It is not difficult to think of factors which might comprise this residual.

Some would lay the blame on the backwardness of British management: its failure to employ sufficient technical expertise and to use modern management techniques. Others see the root of the trouble in restrictive labour practices. Others, again, would single out the amateurism of the governmental machine – at both parliamentary and civil-service levels – as a major anti-growth element. There is no shortage of anecdotal evidence to support these alternative views.

But similar material could easily be collected in other economies which have nonetheless managed higher growth rates than we have. Is there any reason why socio-economic factors should play a greater part in Britain than elsewhere?

Perhaps there is. The Brookings Institution report on the out-look for the British economy[2] emphasized the extent to which Britain remains sharply stratified by class. As outside observers, this group of American economists stressed the dilettantism of British industry and the deep-rooted bifurcation of the educational and social system into 'them' and 'us'. If they are right, the result is that British businessmen simply do not take business sufficiently seriously to be as efficient as their counter-parts elsewhere; that British labour, in squabbling about the share-out of the present national cake, retards its further growth; that both are regulated by authorities who lack any real

2. R. E. Caves (ed.), *Britain's Economic Prospects*, Allen & Unwin, 1968.

understanding of either. We fail to grow faster because of the make-up of our social system rather than because of any simple economic deficiency.

Growth and Demand

Another candidate for the part of villain in the piece is the possibility that British governments have been peculiarly bad in creating the *demand* conditions needed to evoke the maximum growth responses from enterprises.

Certainly we have already seen that in the period when Keynesian policies were being applied successive governments felt that to run the economy at a level of demand which would ensure full exploitation of the growth potential might lead to either (a) an acceleration in the rate of inflation or (b) balance of payments difficulties as imports were sucked in at a faster rate than exports were stimulated.

Moreover, it may not just be the overall *level* of demand that is relevant in achieving faster growth, but also its stability. In this respect, the erratic course of economic activity in Britain over the years may well have been an independent source of the slow rate of growth. Stop–go is not very conducive to getting people to adopt attitudes and take decisions likely to increase the growth rate. A general expectation that in the near future there will be a cutback in the level of activity in the economy is not one which encourages forward-looking policies on the part of either business management or trade unions. Uncertainty breeds doubt and suspicion – and a determination to hold on to what they already have rather than a willingness to seek future improvements. Confidence may be an important element in determining the rate of growth of an economy. Assured that sustained growth *will* take place, firms are much more likely to be interested in preparing and implementing long-term investment programmes, in introducing new products and processes; workers, in full-employment conditions of steady growth, may be much more receptive to the idea of changing practices and techniques. Reduction in the uncertainties of the future was one of the aims of the British experiments with 'indicative' planning in the 1960s – the sort of planning which, rather than coercing the various elements in the economy, hoped to bring about changes through mutual consent.

It was argued that if only the *feasibility* of faster growth could be demonstrated – if the various parties could only be shown the *compatibility* of their interests – then we could ultimately *talk* ourselves into a higher growth trend. But the plans failed, partly because the participants in the plans remained unconvinced and preferred to wait and see what the outcome would be, and partly because they were right to remain unconvinced since governments continued to adopt policies which in themselves doomed the plans to failure.

And, of course, if demand *is* a key factor, then the marked deterioration in Britain's growth performance in the late 1970s and early 1980s hardly requires further explanation. It is not surprising to find from a report[3] published in 1983 (a) that in 1982 British manufacturing industry was producing at 15 per cent below even its much diminished capacity; (b) that British companies spent only half as much per employee on research and development compared to other major European industrial nations and that Britain was second from bottom in the O.E.C.D. league for R. and D. spending relative to output; and (c) that allowing for the shorter life of plant and machinery in an age of rapid technological change, Britain had been actually 'disinvesting' (i.e. running *down* its capital stock) since 1980 – by 4 per cent in the first half of 1982 alone.

But there is another, quite different view.

Supply-side Economics

The idea that the key to faster growth lies in manipulating the level of demand in the economy is decisively rejected by monetarists who, as we have seen, do not believe that governments can 'manage' demand without inflationary consequences.

3. O.E.C.D.

For them, the solution to the growth puzzle lies in a combination of first squeezing inflation out of the system by monetary discipline, and then 'freeing' the economy from obstacles inhibiting the efficient working of the market mechanism. 'Supply-side' economists of this persuasion single out governments and trade unions as their prime targets.

Take for instance the labour market. Such supply-side economists argue that the labour market is no different to any other market – like for instance the market for bananas or the market for computers. We have already examined their view that if unemployment exists, it is because wages must be too high. The policy implication of this for a government wanting lower unemployment is that it must encourage a reduction in wages and encourage a willingness to work. Yet, it is argued, many government policies do the reverse of this. 'High' levels of unemployment benefits encourage workers to stay on the dole. Government-established bodies setting wage rates for the low-paid in industries such as retailing or hairdressing (known as 'wage councils') encourage unemployment by setting 'high' minimum wages for the industry. The law of the land gives trade unions the power to take industrial action with relative impunity. The balance of power between workers and their employers has tilted too much in favour of the worker. And there is a considerable 'hidden' wage to be paid in the form of payroll taxes on employees (in Britain, national insurance employers' contribution), pension costs, costs of subsidized facilities such as canteens, sickness benefits and all the expenditure on health and safety at work imposed by governments not thinking of the consequent burden to industry. On this argument, the way to improve the functioning of the labour market is to cut unemployment benefits, introduce anti-union legislation, reduce payroll taxes on industry and abolish much of the legislation passed in the 1960s and 1970s designed to enhance the rights of workers at work.

Earlier chapters have sought to cast doubt on many of these ideas. Would wage cuts in fact solve the unemployment problem – even though reduced wages would lead to less spending and still fewer orders for industry? Are unemployment benefits in fact high enough to deter any but a tiny minority from taking a job if available? And most important of all, in all this striving for 'efficiency' have we totally lost sight of efficiency 'for whom?' If by an efficient economy we mean one where unemployment is the norm for a significant minority of the population, where lack of work results in hopeless poverty, where a significant proportion of those in work have such low wages that they are unable to benefit from the affluent society in which we live, where workers are expected to work in unsafe and unhealthy conditions and be thankful for it, then surely we have ceased to live in a civilized society. We must always remind ourselves that an economy must serve the needs of society as a whole – society must not be the slave of its economic system.

Another major obstacle to growth, according to such economists, are barriers to entrepreneurship. The entrepreneur is a person who risks his own money in setting up and running a firm. High rates of tax, government red tape and the power of unions, it is claimed, may all discourage the entrepreneur. Furthermore, *small* firms have received increasing attention as an important source of innovative entrepreneurship. During the 1960s the gradual concentration of production in the hands of *larger* firms had been positively encouraged by government in the belief that efficiency and productivity depended on mass production. In 1966, the Labour government under Harold Wilson established the Industrial Reorganization Corporation (I.R.C.) to encourage the mergers of firms which, it was felt, were too small to compete on the world markets or even in the British market. Abolished in 1971, the I.R.C. represented a high-water mark for the 'big is beautiful' school of economic thought. But in the 1970s the importance of the small firm came to be more and more emphasized. It was argued that large firms were often inefficient because they lacked the pressure of competition. And since 1979, a mass of legislation encouraging small firms has been put on the statute-book, mostly related to tax concessions or grants for new entrepreneurs. On the face of it, it seems to have worked. New company registrations have been steadily rising since 1974. In 1982, approximately 125,000 new companies were registered. However, it is also the case that since 1979, the number of company liquidations has risen at a similar rate. In 1982, 118,000 companies 'died' for one reason or another. That only left a net increase in 1982 of 7,000 companies. Considering these figures, it becomes plain that, as yet, new small companies are not making much positive contribution to reducing unemployment or increasing output.

Central to this type of supply-side argument is the idea that growth depends upon competitiveness. 'Leaner and fitter' was a phrase much used in the early 1980s to rationalize the great shake-out in manufacturing industry then taking place. Certainly, many parts of British industry up to the late 1970s had been consistently less efficient than their main trading rivals. This partly accounts for the gradual decline in our percentage share of world markets and the increase in import penetration by our international competitors. The economic climate of the early 1980s was to be an ideal proving-ground for the attempt to make British industry leaner. High interest rates, increased taxes, cuts in government capital spending, and a high pound all contributed to the 14 per cent decline in manufacturing output experienced between 1979 and the second quarter of 1983. Labour productivity – output per man – increased dramatically over these years. Thus between 1980 and 1982, it rose by no less than 11 per cent, a remarkable advance given that it had only increased by 22 per cent over the seven years from 1975 to 1982. Some of the increase has undoubtedly come from improved working practices. By 1979, there were still far too many examples of restrictive practices – of men unnecessarily employed to perform non-existent tasks. A year later, with industry in the grip of depression, firms were telling their workers that the very survival of their jobs depended upon increased productivity. Workers were given the stark choice of redundancies or changes in work practices and wage freezes or cuts.

However, what was probably of more importance in accounting for the increase in productivity was the wholesale decimation of the weaker parts of industry. Factory after factory was closed. Existing operations were scaled down. By the simple laws of arithmetic, if factories with the lower productivity are closed down, the remainder will on average have a higher productivity level than before. But the increase is to some extent an illusion. As we have said earlier, industry is considerably leaner, but not necessarily fitter. On the contrary, the scaling down of industry to match current levels of output has in an important respect left it weaker than before. The destruction which took place between 1979 and 1982 was of the factories which accounted for much of our ability to respond quickly to an upturn in demand. With these gone, there is a very real danger that any economic revival will result not in expanded domestic output but, even more than before, in an upsurge of imports.

An increase in labour productivity is only one component of a general increase in competitiveness. Has our 'leaner and fitter' industry now got the right environment to invest and innovate? In the sense that competition in most markets today is keener than in the late 1970s, firms have got that incentive. If they fail to produce the right products at the right prices they will be driven out of business.

As yet, there is little sign that British industry is taking the necessary steps to avoid this happening in responding to the increasingly competitive environment by substantial new investment. On the contrary, manufacturing investment has markedly declined since 1979 and firms remain sceptical about the prospects for sustained growth that would warrant them investing for increased production in the future.

Alternative 'Supply-side' Economics

It should not be assumed that 'supply-side' economics is the sole preserve of what can loosely be termed radical right-wing economists. Certainly Keynesians emphasize the importance of a high and stable level of *demand* not only in restoring full employment but in stimulating economic growth. And there may be some who think that would be sufficient in itself to generate investment, improved productivity and more dynamic managerial attitudes.

More commonly, however, buoyant demand is seen as a necessary rather than a sufficient condition for sustained growth – with the need for considerable supplementation on the supply side along lines that are, however, very different from those just outlined. Instead of 'freeing' the operation of market forces, supply-side policies are seen as compensating for the results of 'market failure'. For example, as we saw in Chapter 4, free-market forces are likely to exacerbate rather than solve the problem of regional imbalance: high-quality labour and capital are likely to move from the poorer regions to the richer ones, making it even more difficult for the depressed areas to attract new enterprise. The regional problem can, it is argued, only be cured or even stabilized by positive interventionist measures.

Similarly, it is claimed, even in a climate of expanding demand, improvements in competitiveness may only be elicited by specific policies aimed not only at increasing total investment but by tighter control of the capital market to ensure that such investment is directed into the most nationally productive channels. Planning agreements with private companies in receipt of government grants or tax concessions about the nature of their investment and export programmes, government partnership in key sectors of the economy, and massive public investment in improving the national infrastructure may all be elements in an alternative economic strategy. And if the benefits of renewed growth within a context of new technology are ever to be equitably distributed it is difficult to avoid the conclusion that we shall one day have to reopen the debate on how an effective prices and incomes policy can be introduced.

Such matters are not on the current agenda. For the time being we must await the outcome of the monetarist-cum-market experiment which will have to be judged not simply in terms of its effectiveness or failure in increasing Britain's growth rate but also by the costs that have been involved at a time when North Sea oil seemed to offer the possibility of a breakthrough to higher investment levels without the harsh reduction in consumption that would generally be necessary. It may be that just as we today look back on the 1930s as a time of wasted opportunity and misguided government policy, so in fifty years' time we shall regret the unnecessary sacrifice imposed upon this generation in the 1980s.

9

The Way of the Market

Previous chapters have examined the workings of the economy as a whole – so-called *macro-economics*. We have seen that economists are deeply divided in their understanding of how the economy works, and therefore offer very different answers about which policies are appropriate in solving major problems such as inflation and unemployment. We are now going to turn our attention to *micro-economics* – considering how individual workers, consumers and producers behave, and how resources are allocated within the economy. In this we shall be much concerned with considering the more detailed implications of the macro-economic strategy that has been pursued in recent years.

Micro-economics is as fraught with controversy as macro-economics. Some economists argue that the free-market mechanism is the ideal vehicle for optimizing the provision of goods and services in an economy. High on their list of priorities are increased competition, privatization, and the removal of legal and tax constraints on the operations of private firms. Other economists argue that the free-market mechanism, while having a valuable role to play in the economy, is a very imperfect mechanism. Considerable state intervention is needed to improve its functioning or correct its failures. In this chapter, we will consider how the free-market mechanism is supposed to operate and briefly consider some of its limitations. In later chapters, we will discuss those limitations in more detail.

One of the classic definitions of economics was given by Professor Lionel Robbins in *The Nature and Significance of*

Economic Science (1934), where he described it as: 'The Science which studies human behaviour as a relationship between ends and scarce means which have alternative uses.' This definition, though in some ways unsatisfactory, does serve to emphasize an economic question which over the years has engaged a very large proportion of economists' attention – that of *resource allocation*. This, for many economists, was and still is *the* economic problem.

The first element in the problem is that we have available in an economy only finite quantities of resources. These may be natural – soil, climate, mineral deposits – which are tradition-ally termed Land; they may be man-made – factories, machines, roads, etc. – in which case they are referred to as Capital; and then there is man himself – Labour. Land, Labour and Capital, resources which at any given time are strictly limited in supply. They are also capable of being brought together in various combinations to produce alternative types and quantities of goods and services. We are faced with the 'guns or butter' issue of economic choice: the more resources that are used for one particular form of output, the less there are available for others.

This is the basic economic scene. Enter now the actors them-selves – consumers jostling to get hold of as many goods and services as they can. Whether it is because we are inherently avaricious or whether it is the nature of our economic system which implants high consumption goals, the shopping list of what consumers would like to have is so long that, to all intents and purposes, we may as well say that wants are unlimited. (Note that it is the wants of consumers, rather than the needs, with which economics has traditionally been concerned.)

Scarce resources capable of alternative uses – and infinite con-sumer wants. How can the two be reconciled? The answer is, of course, that they can't. But the aim of economics, according to Robbins, is to make the best of a bad job. The economic problem becomes one of analysing ways of allocating finite resources in such a manner that consumer satisfactions are 'maximized'.

The difficulty is that consumers, except in a very simple

economy (for example the croft, where the crofter is both consumer and producer), have no direct relationship with resources. A linking mechanism is needed if the two are to be brought into contact.

There are two very broad alternatives. The first is to interpose between the consumers and resources a central authority with the responsibility for directly planning the types and quantities of goods and services to be produced. There are various criteria by which it could work. The authority could claim to *know* what consumers wanted; it could try to find out – by trial and error, or through the use of market-research techniques; or it could order the production of those goods and services which it thinks consumers need, or *ought* to want. In the rather unattractive extreme form in which it has been presented here, such a system has won the emotive label of a Command Economy. Without going into further detail for the present, it can at least be said that the system would have a more obvious rationale in a poor economy (where basic needs are fairly easily identifiable) than in a richer economy (where production choices may be between sophisticated goods like televisions and washing machines).

The alternative framework for allocating resources is that of the Market Economy, which relies upon the impersonal workings of the price mechanism to do the job of bringing consumers into contact with resources. The intermediary between the two is the firm, which forges a double link, one backward to resources, through the factor market, and the other forward to consumers, in the market for final goods. A market is simply a meeting of buyers and sellers. In the factor market, the so-called 'factors of production' – land, labour and capital – are offered for sale to the various firms competing for their services. The final goods market is that where consumers make their purchases from the variety of goods and services offered for sale by the firms.

The process has frequently been described as one of economic democracy. Each of the consumers has a limited number of votes, represented by his income. He or she casts these according to his or her tastes, for the various candidates (the goods

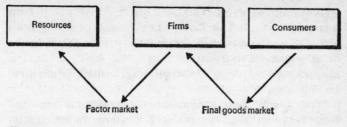

Figure 19

and services on offer) put forward by the firms. The firm is merely a go-between. Having collected the votes, its job is then to re-cast them, on behalf of the consumers, in the market for factors. The more votes it has received from consumers, the greater the quantity of factors it can lay its hands on. For the votes are not an index of the popularity or otherwise of the firms themselves, but rather a signal to them from consumers about how resources should be distributed.

Consumers, it is supposed, have wants far in excess of what their limited incomes can buy. They therefore have to choose. And if they do so calculatingly and rationally (and on the basis of full information about the alternatives available), they will finish up in a position of getting equal satisfaction from the last ten pence which they have spent on each of the products they buy. If that is not the case, it will pay them to substitute some goods for others until it is so. Only then will they be maximizing the satisfaction that can be derived from their incomes, and they will have done so by *marginal* calculations – asking, of each item of consumption, 'how much is this adding to my satisfaction and how much is it costing me?'

Firms are also assumed to be maximizers, but for them it is profits which are the spur. To make the greatest profit possible they too must act marginally. Some units of output would add more to their costs than to their total receipts; they therefore won't produce them. Others, adding more to revenue than costs, are profitable. The golden rule for profit maximization is: expand output to the point at which the last unit produced adds as much to revenue (marginal revenue) as it adds to costs (marginal cost). And similarly, when it comes to inputs, firms will maximize profits when, for example, the last man they take on adds as much to their total wage bill as their total receipts are increased by selling the larger output which results from his employment.

What brings them all into touch – consumers, firms and factors of production – are prices. Prices form the key element in the market system.

The price of anything depends on how much of it is offered for sale (supply) and the amount which people are prepared to buy (demand). The interests of consumers and producers are at odds with each other. Consumers want lower prices and producers try to charge as much as they can. For consumers, the lower the price, the greater generally is the quantity of a product which they are prepared to buy. A typical set of consumers' plans is shown in Fig. 20A – a demand curve showing that the

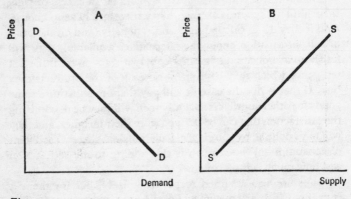

Figure 20

the price the less consumers would be willing to buy. Firms, on the other hand, react in the opposite way. The higher the price which *they* can get, the greater the quantity that they are prepared to put on the market. A simple production plan for an industry is illustrated graphically in the supply curve of Fig. 20B.

The demand and supply curves show just *plans*. They indicate what consumers and firms *would* do if the price were such and such. But how is the actual market price determined? Fig. 21 brings together the two sets of information about demand and supply plans. Quite clearly there is only one price at which plans to produce and plans to consume are compatible. This so-called 'equilibrium' price is the one towards which market forces will always be pressing. If price is higher than that, the amount supplied will exceed the amount demanded. Stocks will pile up in the shops; retailers may cut prices in order to clear them and they will certainly be on the telephone to the manufacturers to reduce their future orders. A lower price, on

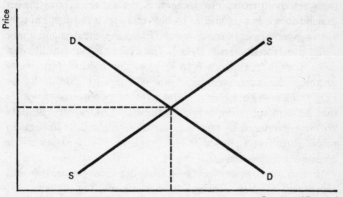

Supply and Demand

Figure 21

the other hand, will be one which generates more demand than there is supply. Either queues will be formed, or retailers may themselves choke off the excess demand by raising prices.

In the ideal market system it is the consumer who calls the tune. Suppose, for example, that there is a switch in taste away from beef and in favour of pork. Fig. 22 shows the effect on

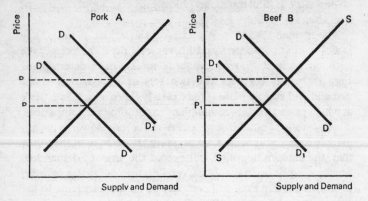

Figure 22

their relative prices. The increased popularity of pork means that housewives are willing to buy more of it than previously at any given price. In other words (Fig. 22A), the demand curve shifts bodily to the right (D_1D_1). The upshot is that equilibrium price of pork rises from P to P_1, and this induces farmers to produce the extra quantity now demanded. Similarly, as Fig. 22B shows, the effect of the reduced popularity of beef is that its demand curve moves to the left (D_1D_1) as consumers are now prepared to buy only smaller amounts at any given price. Equilibrium price falls from P to P_1 – and supply is consequently choked off.

In this way, prices act as a link between consumers and resources. Higher demand by consumers for a particular product will force up its price. The firms getting greater revenue as a result will be able to bid resources – land, labour and capital – away from other firms whose products are less popular. The consumer, despite having no direct contact with factors of production, has nonetheless dictated the way in which they are deployed. The consumer is sovereign. Prices, reflecting consumer demands *and* the relative scarcity of resources in an economy, act as signposts pointing to the way in which those resources should be allocated.

The ideal market system is one in which well-informed consumers make careful and rational choices; producers charge prices enough only to cover costs plus a 'normal' profit just sufficient to keep them in business; and resources can be moved freely from one type of production to another in response to changing consumer demands. Provided that all these conditions are met, the outcome will be an optimum use of resources with consumers being satisfied to the greatest possible extent.

This is the mesmeric appeal of the price mechanism. It allocates resources optimally. And it is beautifully simple. All that is needed is that we be ourselves and pursue our own self-interest. Magically, without any intervention from the authorities, resources are channelled into their most efficient uses.

But does it work in practice? We have already examined one possible defect of fundamental significance: that, according to Keynesians, an unregulated market economy is highly unlikely to yield stable full employment. But does it, in the real world, even guarantee that those resources which *are* employed are used efficiently? There are many grounds for doubt.

If their satisfactions are to be maximized, consumers must act like 'economic men' – coldly calculating, rational and perfectly knowledgeable. Are they really like this, or are they subject to habit and impulse, ignorant of the prices and qualities of goods offered for sale, and easily manipulated and deceived by advertising? Even if consumers as a whole are sovereign, the highly unequal distribution of income and wealth certainly means that some are more sovereign than others; the price mechanism cannot distinguish between a pound spent by a poor man and a pound spent by a rich man, although they may mean very different things.

Then again, it can be argued that consumers are *not*, in practice, sovereign. Firms do not passively respond to their demands, but set out deliberately to mould consumer tastes so that supply creates demand rather than the other way round. The role of profits is a further case where practice may seriously diverge from the ideal. Profits ought to be indicators of efficiency – 'the index of what people want. Where high profits are being made, there is unsatisfied demand and the high profits will attract more capital and more energy into meeting it. Where low profits are being made, capital and energy are being wasted.'[1] But in reality high profits can also arise because firms have achieved a dominant market position in which they can charge high prices with impunity: profits in this case reflect the degree of monopoly rather than competitive efficiency.

Finally, resources in practice are not, as the theory assumes, perfectly mobile. Workers and capital do not move quickly and freely from one line of production to another in response to price signals. And even when market forces do work, they may do so very slowly. A particular industry may be bound to decline in face of falling demand, but its contraction may be long drawn out and painful.

These are all matters which we shall be examining later in the real context of the British economy. But if there is anything in these criticisms of the market economy, then prices are not very reliable or effective signals for allocating resources. The *practical* limitations of the market provide a rationale for government intervention aimed at creating the necessary conditions to make the price mechanism work as it should ideally (for example, by anti-monopoly legislation) or anticipating the outcome of market forces and speeding them up.

So far, we are still assuming that the market system is an appropriate *ideal* which would be acceptable if only its blemishes and imperfections could be removed. But even this way of looking at it is very questionable.

(i) A basic criticism of the market system concerns what is *omitted* from the price calculus. Firms will produce only if their revenue is at least equal to their costs (including an appropriate return to capital). Revenue in excess of costs may induce them to expand production. Revenue below costs will be a sign that they should contract and perhaps ultimately leave an industry altogether under the 'discipline of the market'. All these calculations are naturally internal to the firm. What goes into its

1. E. Powell, *Freedom and Reality*, Batsford, 1969, p. 28.

balance sheet are the costs and the benefits as they appear to that individual production unit.

However, economists have long recognized that these may not represent the whole story. In the course of its production, a firm may bestow on other producers incidental benefits which do not show up on its own balance sheet. And it may impose costs on the economy which it does not itself have to bear. These external or social costs and benefits – genuinely economic though they are – may not be reflected at all in actual market prices which determine the way in which resources are allocated.

We have become increasingly aware of the degree to which private and social costs and benefits may diverge. Closing down a coal-mine in a Scottish village may be perfectly justifiable on the *commercial* grounds that it simply does not pay. But, *economically*, keeping the pit open may be justifiable if the resources involved are highly specific and immobile, so that releasing them from their present use does not mean that they are redeployed in more efficient lines of production. For most people, the criterion of whether something pays is the economic be-all-and-end-all. In fact, it is important that wider costs and benefits are taken into account in determining economic viability.

(ii) A further limitation of the market system is that it may lead to the production of goods generally regarded as undesirable, while at the same time failing to produce goods which are not easily priced. A free market could, for example, lead to the output of hard drugs in response to consumer demands. On the other hand, leaving matters like defence or education to the market is not likely to work very well. Defence must be provided collectively because it is impossible for the market to discriminate between those who would be prepared to pay and those who would not; both would be defended regardless. And many social services cannot be left to the market because they are 'merit' goods – those which we decide *ought* to be provided on a scale perhaps greater than that which people would be prepared to pay for privately.

(iii) The market mechanism may work in a way which most

people would regard as 'unfair'. It can be argued that 'The only point about price, the only usefulness about price, is to indicate the relationship of supply and demand. There is no justice or injustice about it, any more than about the readings on a thermometer or a pressure gauge.'[2] But prices are based on the existing income distribution which many would regard as unsatisfactory, and the operation of the market mechanism perpetuates inequalities which, as will be argued later, have little economic or moral justification.

(iv) To repeat the point made earlier, the market may lead to the economy being in 'equilibrium' with mass unemployment, with attempts to clear the labour market through wage reductions only leading to further redundancies as aggregate demand falls and firms lose orders.

(v) Finally, there are those who would condemn the market system at a philosophical level as being based on uncurbed individualism and exploiting the meaner of human motives.

Certainly, it is in this last very broad framework that discussion about the pros and cons of the market economy are frequently couched. The market mechanism is equated with capitalist free enterprise; the alternative is seen as socialist planning. But is this the real issue?

We must distinguish between the market mechanism as an instrument and as a philosophy. As an instrument, its critics point to its past associations and practical outcome. But these are not intrinsic to the use of prices in allocating resources. The fact that it has been more commonly used in capitalist economies does not mean that it would have no place in a society in which the means of production were publicly owned. It may in the past have led to inequality, instability and an unacceptable pattern of output. But it could be used to achieve quite different results. Until we devise some clear alternative techniques for coping with the enormously complex problems of allocating resources in a modern industrial economy, it remains a vitally useful part of our economic system. Planning need not be a stark alternative to the market system. It could help to make it work

2. Powell, op. cit., p. 28.

more effectively. This would involve not only creating conditions in which the market could function at its neutral best but also building into it whatever values we think important.

A 'free' market system, on the other hand, without such manipulation may well be more akin to applying the law of the economic jungle. Survival is dependent upon the fitness and quick-wittedness of the individual. Those least able to cope – the old, the handicapped, those with few marketable talents, the unemployed – end up with little or no share of the economic prosperity which surrounds them. Those who do well in the system are not encouraged to share their prosperity – after all, there would be no incentive for the unemployed, the general labourer, the handicapped person, the old age pensioner to better themselves if the fruits of economic prosperity were evenly distributed. But is this not a basic negation of what we understand by justice and fairness, leading to an uncaring society where the individual feels no responsibility for the plight of the less well-off?

For most of this century, the free-market mechanism has been in retreat in Britain. The State has gradually assumed greater responsibility for providing goods and services – from medical care to electricity. Markets in the private sector of the economy have become increasingly controlled through legislation and direct state intervention. More recently, however, a vigorous counter-attack has been made by proponents of the free-market mechanism. In 1979, a government was elected promising to roll back the frontier of state provision and state intervention. In the next two chapters we shall consider whether or not the private sector, via a free-market mechanism, really can provide many goods and services as efficiently as the State. Is it true, as free-market proponents claim, that the private sector can provide more choice, better products at less cost than the public sector?

10

The Firm in Theory and Practice

Proponents of the market mechanism argue that it is the most efficient way of deciding how resources should be used by enabling consumers to get the best value they can for their money. In economists' jargon, it leads to an optimal allocation of resources. But as we have just seen, this would only be true if a number of highly unrealistic conditions held good. For example, one such condition is the widespread prevalence of free competition amongst producers – offering extensive consumer choice. If this is not so, then consumer choice is limited to allocating spending 'votes' between only a few, or perhaps to just a single firm – with the possibility that it will pocket some of the votes in monopoly profits rather than pass them on into the factor markets.

In the absence of free competition, there is a radical change in the balance of power between consumer and producer which is postulated in the ideal market model. For now firms have a degree of control over *what products* consumers purchase, *what price* they pay – and even *how much* they consume. Profit, instead of being an indicator of how scarce resources should be allocated, becomes a measure of the power of the producer over the consumer. In this chapter, we will argue that free competition, far from being a norm, is the exception in the British economy. If this is so, then the ability of the free-market mechanism to provide us efficiently with goods and services must be seriously questioned. In particular, is there any justification for transferring public industries and services to a private sector where competition is so limited?

The textbook picture of the firm is of a single-plant, single-product enterprise run by single-minded 'entrepreneurs' with the sole object in life of maximizing profits. The theory then portrays firms such as these in a variety of industrial settings. The first is that of perfect competition, a situation with two main features. There are a large number of buyers and sellers each too small independently to influence the market price. And there is free entry into the industry. In perfect competition, the firm is said to be a price-taker.

To see what is meant by this, take the case of a market gardener in, say, Bedfordshire (and also suppose that there are no such things as Marketing Boards). Early each morning, a lorry from a local haulage firm calls to take his lettuces for sale at Covent Garden. The producer does not tell the lorry driver how much he wants for the lettuces; it is left to him to get the best price he can. The price which he *does* get depends entirely on the situation in Covent Garden on any particular day. There, lettuces will be coming in from a large number of different sources, and they will be bought by many independent wholesalers, hotels and so on. The actual market price on that day will be one which balances supply and demand. Suppose, for example, that it settles at 10p per lettuce. Then, if the market gardener had instructed the lorry driver to accept no less than 11p, he would have sold none, because one lettuce is much like another and nobody would have bought his more expensive produce. On the other hand, he would have been foolish to ask for only 6p when the going rate turned out to be 10p. The best he can do is to take what the market offers.

The great theoretical attraction of the perfectly competitive combination of price-taking and free entry is that it yields an outcome in which prices and profits are pushed down to minimum levels. If profits happen temporarily to rise above a 'normal' level (defined as that which is just sufficient to keep firms in their present line of business) then the result will be that new firms are attracted into the industry. The consequent increase in supply coming onto the market depresses price and eliminates the excess profits of the original group of producers.

This is the reason why the perfectly competitive model has

retained such an appeal for economists for the century and a half since it was first formulated. Indeed, at that time it could be said to have roughly fitted the facts of the British economy, consisting as it did mostly of small owner-enterprises. The enormous structural changes which have subsequently taken place in the economy have rendered the model largely useless as a description of reality. But economic theorists, aware of this, have nonetheless continued to view perfect competition as the yardstick for measuring deviations from the ideal.

Thus, in a typical textbook of the pre-1930 vintage, lengthy discussion of the merits of perfect competition would be followed by the entry of the villain – monopoly, or the absence of competition. Monopoly occurred when the output of a good was completely dominated by a single producer. In this case, the firm *was* the industry. The effect, as could be shown by intricate geometrical diagrams, was that the monopolist – by restricting output and raising prices – could earn abnormal profits over and above those necessary to keep him in business. Moreover, it was claimed that monopolies, lacking a competitive stimulus, tended to be inefficient in other ways. They lacked the incentive to innovate and management became sluggish.

However, instances of monopoly – in the sense of complete absence of competition – are as difficult to find as perfect competition. During the 1930s, therefore, an attempt to add realism to the theory was made by the introduction of a new concept – 'monopolistic competition', or 'imperfect competition' as it became known, which was neither monopoly nor competition but combined elements of both. Most firms, it was argued, although competing with many others, did so primarily through advertising and other forms of product differentiation. Shirt producers, for example, each would be trying to give his product a distinctive design, fashion or packaging which would attract consumer loyalty. To begin with, the firms in such an industry might make excess profits, but new firms would then set up in business and whittle them away. However, in the process excess capacity would be created in the original firms as they now had to share the market with a greater number of rivals. This tendency to chronic excess capacity is one of the main predictions of imperfect competition analysis – and something akin to it can perhaps be seen in the retail trade.

The extension of the theory of the firm to accommodate problems of imperfect competition was nonetheless very much within the traditional analytical framework. The firms' single-minded pursuit of profit maximization was still assumed. And it still allowed the individual firm to be studied in isolation from others. This was possible because, under conditions of perfect and imperfect competition, each firm was too small for its activities to have any noticeable effect on the price and output decisions of others; nor, in turn, was it influenced by any other firm's policies. And in monopoly, effects on rivals could of course be ignored because there were no rivals.

But just how great a step towards realism did the new analysis represent? More broadly, how well can the traditional theory of the firm as a whole explain what happens in the real world?

In a modern industrial economy isolated instances can be found which do roughly approximate to perfect competition or monopoly. And the majority of firms probably operate in situations rather like imperfect competition. So far so good. But a substantial and growing proportion of output, and the bulk of industrial production, comes from firms in industries which can be classified under none of these headings. Undoubtedly, the most important market situation today is that of oligopoly. Oligopoly is competition between the few – and the few are typically very large-scale enterprises who between them dominate an industry.

It is at just this point that traditional economic theory becomes least helpful. It offers very little indeed by way of explanation of oligopolistic behaviour. The principal reason for its failure to throw any light on the matter is the methodology of analysing a firm in isolation from others, which works in the cases of perfect and imperfect competition and monopoly but which completely breaks down in the case of oligopoly. That is because, when there are only a few large rivals in an industry, the *essence* of the problem is their uncertainty about rivals' reactions to their own policies. Oligopoly is above all featured by interdependence of rivals' pricing and output decisions. The biggest question mark for Firm X, contemplating a price rise for its product, is how Firms Y and Z will react. Will they just match the price increase, raise prices by a smaller amount, keep their prices the same or lower prices? Without this information, which is not available, Firm X cannot predict what its sales will be at the higher price. And, if it goes ahead with its price rise, Firm X in turn will have to decide how to respond to the reactions of Firms Y and Z.

It is precisely these dynamics of interdependence which traditional theory is unable to handle. Attempts have been made to make the analysis of oligopolistic situations more manageable by making assumptions about rivals' reactions. Some early theorists even went so far as to assume that rivals would not react at all. That certainly enabled them to formulate determinate conclusions about oligopolistic pricing and output policies, but only, of course, at the cost of assuming away the oligopolistic problem itself! Others have argued that reactions will be asymmetrical – that price rises will not be followed by rivals, whereas price cuts will. This, they suggest, makes for price stability in oligopolistic situations, with competition diverted to product differentiation, innovation and general service competition. Others again have sought an explanation of oligopolistic behaviour by postulating price leadership or evolving complex strategical options based on the mathematical theory of games.

One leading economist warns his readers that 'there is no single well-developed theory of the functioning of oligopolistic markets'. He goes on to say 'in our introductory treatment of this subject we have come very close to one of the frontiers of modern economics'.[1] Put another way, we simply do not know how to explain the most important part of a modern industrial economy.

Nearly every major industry today – cars, oil, chemicals,

1. R. G. Lipsey, *Introduction to Positive Economics*, 5th edn, Weidenfeld & Nicolson, 1979, pp. 283 and 288.

tobacco, electricals – is dominated by a handful of giant companies. In Britain, the share of the largest 100 firms rose from less than 20 per cent of net output in the economy before the First World War to 33 per cent in 1958, and to nearly 50 per cent by 1970.[2] And the process of industrial concentration continues. Spending on take-overs during the first half of the 1960s was something like ten times that of the 1950s. By 1970, £2,597m. of assets were involved in merger or take-over deals. By 1980, this had risen tenfold to £21,964m. (These figures are only for merger activities involving more than £5m. worth of assets – approximately 20 per cent of all mergers by number.) There seems to be no limit to the process. Of the top ten British companies rated by the *Financial Times* in October 1982, six had engaged in significant merger activity in the previous twenty years. These companies were General Electric Company (G.E.C.), Beecham Group, British American Tobacco (B.A.T.) Industries, Grand Metropolitan, Barclays Bank and Great Universal Stores. Of the other four, British Petroleum, Shell Transport and Trading, Imperial Chemical Industries and Marks and Spencer, only Marks and Spencer can be said to be a company which has no interest in merger activity.

What lies behind this concentration of industry into larger and larger enterprises? The stock answer of economists and of the businesses themselves is that size is a necessary condition for achieving what are called economies of large-scale production. In many industries, higher production levels allow substantial cuts to be made in unit costs.

For example, one study showed that total cost per unit in brick production would rise by 25 per cent compared to the lowest possible cost if production took place in a plant half the lowest cost size.[3] In the motor-car industry, 'Something like a 40 per cent reduction in costs can be expected as production increases from 1,000 to 50,000 units per annum. Doubling volume to 100,000 units should lower costs by 15 per cent; while

2. S. J. Prais, *The Evolution of Giant Firms in Great Britain: A study of concentration in manufacturing industry in Britain 1909–1970*, C.U.P., 1976.

3. C. F. Pratten, *Economies of Scale in Manufacturing Industry*, C.U.P., 1971.

a further doubling to 200,000 should achieve another 10 per cent in savings. The jump to 400,000 yields an additional 5 per cent, and expansion beyond this point results in progressively smaller savings for each additional 100,000, the gains tapering off at a level of about 1,000,000.'[4] 'The Boeing 747 (Jumbo Jet) airliner, which is about two and a half times the size of the 707 airliner and carries about 390 passengers compared with about 140, is said to be 20–30 per cent cheaper in terms of direct operating costs per passenger.'[5]

All of these are examples of technical economies of scale. The large firm, because it can spread its overheads over a long production run, can often use superior techniques to its smaller rival, or achieve economies by installing a larger version of the same techniques, or combine techniques in a more efficient way. But in addition to technical economies there are a number of other advantages accruing to a large firm.

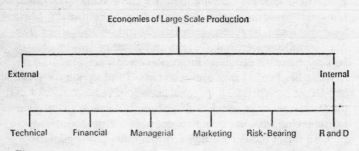

Figure 23

External economies are those which a firm enjoys because of the growth of an industry – the fact, for example, that it will pay other firms to set up to provide it with component parts or use its waste products as a raw material. Financially, the large firm may have access to sources like the Stock Exchange not available to the small firm, and it may be able to borrow at lower

4. G. Maxcy and A. Silbertson, *The Motor Industry*, Allen & Unwin, 1959, p. 93.
5. G. Bannock, *The Juggernauts*, Weidenfeld & Nicolson, 1971, p. 113.

rates. Managerial economies arise with specialization at the boardroom level and the employment of expertise and management aids like computers. On the marketing side, the large firm may be able to control its own distribution network and use mass media advertising to a greater extent. And through diversification it can spread its risks over a wide range of products.

All of these are essentially static advantages. But on top of these there is an important dynamic economy of scale in that the larger enterprise is able to devote a greater amount to research and development – from which, it hopes, new products and processes will emerge. In other words, the large firm not only holds all the aces now; it is also in a better position to develop in the future.

There is no denying the very real significance of economies of scale. On the other hand, it is easy to exaggerate them. First of all, advantages of size differ from industry to industry. The optimum size of plant may be large in the motor-car industry but relatively small in, for example, the production of motor-car tyres. Secondly, in addition to economies there may be diseconomies of scale; in particular there are the difficulties of running very large enterprises, which modern computerized techniques of management can only partially overcome.

But what is really doubtful is how far the degree of concentration in modern industrial economies can in any case be attributed to the dictates of technology. It is difficult to see what significant economies of scale could result from many recent mergers and take-overs. Indeed the Monopolies Commission, since it was given powers to investigate them, has on occasion rejected prospective mergers on just this ground. Then again, particularly in the case of technical economies, it is the size of *plant* rather than the size of firm which counts. And yet many very large companies have made little apparent effort to consolidate their production into fewer factories. Furthermore, much growth of firms has taken place through the acquisition of firms engaged in quite different lines of business; no obvious economies result, for example, from a cigarette manufacturer taking over a potato-crisp producer.

Evidence suggests that mergers have relatively little impact on company profitability.[6] If that is so, and if it is also true that most of the present industrial giants have grown to a point far beyond any technological imperatives, then clearly we must ask some fundamental questions about what makes them tick.

Economic theory assumes that firms are profit-maximizers and that profits are an index of efficiency leading to movements of capital from one line of production to another. Both these propositions are questionable.

The Profit Motive. Doubt about whether firms are solely motivated by profit maximization stems principally from their changed institutional nature, first charted in the 1930s by Berle and Means and James Burnham.[7] Nearly all major firms and joint-stock companies are owned by shareholders but run by a board of directors. This divorce of ownership from control means that managerial and owner interests may not entirely coincide. Shareholders, no doubt, *are* solely interested in maximizing profits. But, because of their number, passiveness and lack of knowledge of the complex day-to-day operations of a giant corporation, they are in no position to *know* whether profits are being maximized or not.

None of this is to argue that private firms have lost interest in profits. But there may be a difference between maintaining a high and 'satisfactory' level of profits (enough to keep share-holders quiet and to provide capital for further expansion) and *maximizing* them. It is here that other motivations can be inserted. But what might they be?

Writers like Marris and Galbraith[8] emphasize that it is the managers or 'technostructure' who dominate the boards of large

6. A. Hughes and A. Singh, 'Takeovers in the United Kingdom', in D. C. Mueller (ed.), *Determinants and Effects of Mergers: an international comparison*, Oelgeschlager, Gunn and Hain, 1980.

7. A. A. Berle and G. C. Means, *The Modern Corporation and Private Prosperity*, New York, 1933; and J. Burnham, *The Managerial Revolution*, New York, 1941.

8. R. Marris, *The Economic Theory of Managerial Capitalism*, Macmillan, 1964; and J. K. Galbraith, *The New Industrial State*, Penguin Books, 1969.

companies rather than owners or owner nominees. Not themselves being profit earners, what they may be more concerned with are matters of respectability, status and security. Thus growth of the firm and its diversification into a range of different industries is important for a number of reasons. It enables the firm to achieve a dominant market position in which it is no longer threatened by competition. Its size enhances the status of the managers themselves. Its multiplicity of activities ensures its long-term survival as an ongoing permanent institution. And size can, for the corporation man, become an end in itself.

For Galbraith in particular, what this amounts to is that capitalism today has become a very different animal. The technostructure into whose hands control has largely passed is not only amenable to influence from the State: it positively welcomes it. No longer is there a conflict between State and private industry, because both aim at reducing future uncertainties through planning.

But has the leopard really changed its spots? Certainly the emergence of a powerful managerial class makes it possible to inject motivations other than profit maximization. But how far that has already happened is doubtful. Firstly, many of the 'new' motives which it is suggested now exist can be seen not as conflicting with profit maximization but as a shift in emphasis to *long-run* profit maximization. And, secondly, studies which have been made suggest that *owner* control persists to a remarkable degree. Michael Barratt Brown, for example, found that when he studied the top 120 companies 'about a third had boards consisting mainly of the owner and his family or nominees'.[9] In the United States, '*Fortune* reported that in 1966, controlling ownership of 150 of the 500 largest U.S. corporations rested in the hands of an individual or of the members of a single family'.[10]

9. M. Barratt Brown, *What Economics is About*, Weidenfeld & Nicolson, 1970, pp. 149–50.

10. Quoted in Bob Erith, *A Galbraithian Reappraisal: The Ideological Gadfly*, reprinted in E. K. Hunt and Jesse G. Schwartz, *A Critique of Economic Theory*, Penguin Modern Economics Readings, 1972.

Closer to the truth, then, is probably Marris's assertion that although capitalism today is 'overwhelmingly managerial there nonetheless remains a sufficient number of traditional capitalists to be capable of significantly influencing the managers' behaviour'.

Profits and Efficiency. Profits, in the market model, perform the function of signalling switches of capital from one line of production to another – from inefficient to efficient uses. But in the real world of firms holding dominant market positions and being reluctant to engage in open price competition, they are in a position where they fix their own prices rather than accept them from the market. They are price-makers rather than price-takers and can continue to make high profits even when they are inefficient. In other words, profits may indicate the degree to which they have established a monopoly position rather than how effectively they are using resources.

To sum up then, British industry, far from being made up of large numbers of small firms, run by single-minded 'entrepreneurs' whose sole object in life is to maximize short-run profit, is in fact dominated by a small number of relatively large companies run by managers and directors with a variety of objectives including long-run profit maximization. Profits may still sometimes signal an appropriate reallocation of resources in response to consumer dictates, but often are rather an indicator of the degree of dominance enjoyed by a company in its industry.

Recently, there has been much debate about whether or not the public sector is as efficient as the private sector. Absence of the profit motive in the public sector, it is argued, weakens the incentive of firms to reduce costs or supply the best-quality products to the market. However, in the light of what we have seen in this chapter, it is debatable whether the private sector is genuinely more cost- or product-efficient. Private firms pursue other goals than simple profit maximization. Competition, if it exists at all, may well lead to higher costs in the form of duplication of facilities, heavy advertising outlay, and other selling costs.

Take, for instance, the National Health Service or state education, where it is not at all obvious that the result of privatization would be lower-cost provision. There are a number of reasons for this. Duplication of resources and higher administrative expenditure could be sources of increased costs in an extended private health sector. For instance, two private hospitals in close proximity might each have expensive high-technology equipment that is only used part of the time – which is unlikely to occur in a unified national health service. In a recent report, the O.E.C.D. found that in fact the N.H.S. spent less on administration than most other health-care systems.[11] Equally, if parents have a choice of two private schools, one proving relatively unpopular, then there will be spare capacity at one school while temporary or permanent classrooms are erected at large cost in the other. Kent County Council has repeatedly had to shelve plans for greater choice of schools – where parents would be issued with 'vouchers' equivalent to the standard cost of a state education which could then be 'spent' at any state or private school – partly because of the sheer cost of administering the scheme.

Another reason why privatization might lead to dearer services is, of course, the profit that is naturally sought by private-sector providers. We forget all too often that collective consumption goods are provided at cost to the taxpayer. In contrast, the current expansion of private medical care in Britain is in part being promoted by groups of doctors or financial institutions who recognize full well the potential profit to be made by setting up private hospitals. As a stock-performance review of one major American investor-owned hospital corporation put it: 'management is encouraged by the high profit margins of existing facilities in England.'[12] Privatization could well lead also to higher earnings for some of the staff engaged in providing medical care – because of the different private insurance system

11. O.E.C.D., 'Public Expenditure: Health', Paris, 1978.
12. Quoted in John G. Larson, 'The Role of Private Enterprise in Providing Health Care: the Lessons of the American Experience', *National Westminster Bank Quarterly Review*, November 1980.

by which it would be financed. Hospitals and doctors would thus charge their patients who in turn would get their health insurance company to pay the bill. There is far more opportunity under this type of system for medical staff to earn more through pushing up medical insurance premiums than under a state system where government is accountable for money spent. As one expert has put it: 'capitalists are the enemies of capitalism; always and everywhere they conspire to acquire monopoly power so that they can influence the price, quantity and quality of the product (health care in this case) and ensure that consumer preferences are subordinate to producer (doctor) preferences.'[13]

And when we look at the performance of state-owned industries such as British Steel or British Leyland from the mid-1970s onwards, it is difficult to argue that private industry would have done a better job at reducing manpower, rationalizing markets and turning round what were highly unprofitable firms. After all, if it had not been for the appalling management of British Leyland in the 1960s and early 1970s, this flagship of private industry would never have needed to be taken over as a bankrupt company by the State in the first place. British Leyland and British Steel are both very good examples of companies where it was the quality of management and investment that determined its success or otherwise. The fact that it was owned by the public sector rather than by the private sector, or vice versa, was to that extent irrelevant to performance. It is at other relative merits of private- and public-sector provision that we shall look in more detail in Chapter 11.

13. Alan Maynard, adapting one of Adam Smith's dicta in 'Privatising the National Health Service', *Lloyds Bank Review*, April 1983.

11

Free to Choose?

The twentieth century has seen a tremendous increase in the proportion of national resources controlled by the State – particularly in the period since the Second World War. Major industries were taken into public ownership, the basis of the Welfare State was established and by the 1960s the major political parties were vying for electoral favours with promises of ever wider provision of public services.

By the end of the 1970s, some 30 per cent of U.K. output of goods and services was accounted for by the public sector. In addition there was growing expenditure on state 'transfer payments' from one section of the community to another – such as old age pensions or social security benefits.

The years since 1979 have seen a dramatic attempt to reverse this trend, with governments vigorously committed to 'rolling back the public sector'. A new word – 'privatization' – took its graceless place in the English vocabulary and by the mid-1980s government was hellbent on providing practical illustrations of what it meant.

Several arguments have been put forward to support this radical rightward shift in policy. In Chapter 10 we have already briefly questioned the glib assertion that privatization 'represents the most effective means of extending market forces, and in turn of improving efficiency'.[1]

We now turn to other arguments for reducing the size of the public sector – in particular that greater private-sector production and provision enhance consumer choice and allocate

1. Lord Cockfield, quoted in Economic Progress Report, May 1982.

resources in a pattern of output more attuned to consumer dictates.

In this chapter we examine the validity of such claims and whether the advantages of increased private provision, to the extent that they exist at all, outweigh the loss of welfare that is likely to arise from ignoring important social costs and benefits.

We start with a eulogistic account of how the market mechanism gives to consumers the widest possible freedom of choice, supplied by Enoch Powell:

> The free enterprise economy is the true counterpart of democracy: it is the only system which gives everyone a say. Everyone who goes into a shop and chooses one article rather than another is casting a vote in the economic ballot box: with thousands or millions of others that choice is signalled to production and investment and helps to mould the world just a tiny fraction nearer to people's desire. In this great and continuous general election of the free economy nobody, not even the poorest, is disenfranchised: we are all voting all the time. Socialism is designed on the opposite pattern: it is designed to prevent people getting their own way, otherwise there would be no point in it.[2]

On this view, the N.H.S. 'disenfranchises' and prevents 'people getting their own way' over a range of important choices. Thus consumers are not able to choose which doctor will perform a serious operation, whether they occupy a single bedroom or are in a ward, or the timing of their medical treatment. If on the other hand the health service were in private hands, consumers could consult as many doctors as they wished, could choose their hospital and hospital bedroom, and even the standard of meals they require. Waiting lists would be unknown because the private sector would allocate resources to treating such patients, providing of course that they were willing to pay. In this free market, the consumers would decide what money they wanted to spend on health care and how that money would be spent. Instead of a common service for all patients regardless of their wishes, consumers could decide whether to go for a de luxe service or for a more 'economy' version.

2. E. Powell, op. cit., p. 33.

There are very many reasons for doubting whether this is a proper account of the alternatives. But before turning to the question of whether privatization would increase consumer choice, we should first ask how far such choice already prevails in the existing private sector? To what extent does the textbook picture of consumer sovereignty accord with reality?

To get to the truth of the matter, we begin by looking at consumers themselves and asking how closely they resemble the 'economic man' of traditional theory.

What's Left of Consumer Sovereignty?

Clearly we are not all as rational, consistent and precisely calculating as consumers are in the textbooks. But then the theory never purported to be a straightforward description of reality; it was intended as a highly stylized account of what actually happened. Provided that a fair proportion of consumers act very broadly in the way in which the theory suggests, the fact that the rest of us are careless, irrational and inconsistent need not affect the issue. Given that a good deal of consumption is undertaken by housewives on behalf of the family unit, the theoretical assumptions about consumers do not seem far wrong; a large number of buyers *are* very much aware of what is on offer, do shop around to get the best value they can for their money.

But, however much they take the trouble, it is increasingly difficult for consumers in the real world to meet another requirement of the theoretical model: that they should be perfectly knowledgeable about what they are buying. In an affluent society an increasing proportion of incomes is spent on expensive consumer durable goods like cars, washing machines, televisions, refrigerators and tape recorders. These are all technologically very sophisticated products about which it is difficult to be well informed. Most people simply lack the technical knowledge to be able to decide rationally whether one brand of a product is a better or worse buy than another. The Consumers Association provides a regular flow of information through *Which?* and its associated publications, but only to a limited clientele – who may, incidentally, be those who are already relatively well informed and least in need of it.

To make matters worse, these complex consumer durables are major items of expenditure which recur only at infrequent intervals. Buy a tin of soup which you discover to be tasteless and you can transfer to another brand at once. But by the time the car which has been continuously unsatisfactory becomes due for replacement the model has been succeeded by another about which we are as ignorant as we were about its predecessor.

Another gap between theory and reality emerges when we look at the consumers in their relations with others. Theory investigates the behaviour of the consumer in isolation; in principle, the consumer could be shut up in a room and draw up a list of wants in order of preference. In fact consumption takes place in a social context. What consumers want depends partly on what other consumers already have or are thinking of getting. We must keep up with the Joneses or, better still, be one step ahead of them. This is what economists term the 'demonstration effect'. And on top of this is purely conspicuous consumption: goods bought, not so much for the satisfaction of using them, but because they are useful indicators of social status.

This interdependence of consumption decisions, although it renders a good deal of traditional theory irrelevant, is not in itself a limitation on consumer sovereignty in the same way that consumer ignorance is. But they both make it easier for sovereignty to be eroded from another quarter. Ignorance, vanity and envy all help to make the consuming public very susceptible to manipulation by producers. In theory, firms are passive agents waiting for consumer demands to come through the pipeline. In practice, what is to stop them *creating* demands which they can then profitably satisfy? Does demand create supply in the real world according to what Galbraith calls 'the accepted sequence'?[3] Or do giant companies now impose a

3. J. K. Galbraith, op. cit., pp. 216–17.

'revised sequence' in which supply creates its own demand? They certainly have both the motive and the means to do so.

First, the motive. Modern industrial production is technologically highly complex and involves massive capital outlays on research, pilot projects and the tooling-up of factories. The cost can be recouped only if these enormous overheads can be spread over a very large volume of sales. Given these technological imperatives, argues Galbraith, giant firms simply cannot afford to introduce a product just hoping that the demand will be there on the off-chance that it may be a success. 'Technology, with its companion commitment of time and capital, means that the needs of consumers must be anticipated – by months or years. When the distant day arrives the consumer's willingness to buy may well be lacking ... The needed action ... is evident: in addition to deciding what the consumer will want and will pay, the firm must take every feasible step to see that what it decides to produce is wanted by the consumer at a remunerative price.'[4] They must *create* a market and be as sure as possible that consumers *will* be receptive to their new product. With the degree of advanced commitment which modern technological processes involve firms find it far too risky 'to rely on the untutored responses of the consumer'.[5]

Nor need they do so, for the means of reducing the uncertainties of the market are at hand. Advertising, sales promotion, market research and public relations are now all highly developed techniques. Their effectiveness has been greatly increased by the advent of commercial broadcasting. Big business in themselves, advertising and sales promotion account for nearly 3 per cent of the gross national product. What is left of consumer sovereignty under continuous bombardment from the marketing men?

In some ways advertising is positively beneficial to consumer interests. Some advertising is almost wholly informative and all advertising involves the transmission of *some* information. To this extent, consumers' knowledge of alternatives is increased

4. Galbraith, op. cit., p. 33.
5. ibid., p. 34.

and they can make more rational choices. Classified advertisements – like the small ads in the newspapers – account for nearly
20 per cent of total spending in this field; clearly most of these
serve a perfectly useful function of bringing buyers and sellers
together. On the other hand, a good deal of large-scale
advertising contains extraordinarily little hard fact. It chiefly
consists of emphasizing the name of the company and extolling
the virtues of the product in the most general terms; looking
back at the advertisements of bygone days suggests that the
informative content of advertising has markedly diminished.

But advertising and other marketing techniques also seek to
persuade. In this role they can erode consumer sovereignty in
a variety of ways. The consumer may, for example, be deceived
by advertising. Trouble is in store for advertisers who deliberately falsify the facts. But there is no law to stop them suggesting
that some actually minor product difference is a major reason
why consumers should buy Brand X rather than Brand Y. Customers may be seduced by advertising into impulse buys which
they later regret. And they may be lured into an initial purchase
of a product the consumption of which subsequently becomes
habitual, so that their future range of choice is limited: cigarette
smoking is the obvious example.

However, the major charge against modern marketing
methods is that they work not so much to enable producers to
respond to consumers' *given* wants as actually to engender new
wants. It is the producer tail which wags the consumer dog.
There is a lot in this, although the case rests on a rather uneasy
distinction between 'spontaneous' wants, which somehow
reside in the consumers themselves, and 'manipulated' wants,
which are artificially created by sales promotion. It is not easy to
identify the difference in practice because, as A. P. Lerner has
put it, 'In a rich society like ours, only a very tiny part of what
people want is determined by their physical and chemical make-
up. Almost all their needs and desires are built on observation
and imitation.'[6]

6. A. P. Lerner, 'The Economics and Politics of Consumer Sovereignty',
American Economic Review Papers and Proceedings, May 1972, p. 258.

Product innovation is continually opening up new prospects which consumers previously did not know were even technically feasible. Before television was invented people did not demand moving pictures in their homes because there was no point in them doing so. But once television became available, consumer demand built up rapidly. Had producers created a new want? Or had they merely satisfied the *latent* desires of consumers?

It is possible to find some supporting evidence for this latter view in the fact that firms spend large sums in investigating the potential demand for their products before launching them. 'Available studies indicate that most products that product-development departments regard as "technically successful developments" are never launched on the market because of negative results in market research and market tests.'[7] Producers, it seems, do still take into account what their customers want. And consumers can always say no. 'The scanty evidence available suggests that a very large fraction of the products that are actually launched on markets fail, despite often extensive advance market studies. A rather usual comment in the literature is that between one-third and one-half of all products put on the market are considered failures by the sponsoring firms, in the sense that they withdraw the product from the market within one year.'[8]

However, this view that producers use modern marketing techniques simply to react more sensitively to consumers' own desires ignores the extent to which consumers are already prisoners of the commercial environment dominated by giant industrial companies. Consumers are themselves the product of an ethos in which they have been encouraged to aim at the acquisition of ever greater quantities of goods and services. And within this general pressure towards greater consumption firms then compete by working on the *weaknesses* of consumers: the fact that they *are* more responsive to irrational persuasion than hard information, and that their vanity, envy and insecurity

7. A. Lindbeck, *The Political Economy of the New Left. An Outsider's View*, Harper & Row, 1971, p. 43.

8. ibid.

make them easy and willing victims of manipulation. It is the big industrial producers who set the pace, and the result is a far cry from the economist's simple model of consumer behaviour, in which, generally, the theory is described in terms of 'commodities – bread, tea, oranges, salt, sugar – which are produced outside the industrial system or for which the management of demand is peculiarly difficult'.[9]

The view that consumer sovereignty in the private sector has been totally usurped is exaggerated – but consumer choice in the marketplace is certainly severely limited. For example, with greater private health-care provision, would consumers have enough knowledge to choose between a good doctor and a bad doctor, a good hospital and a bad hospital? Information would almost inevitably be circumstantial and anecdotal. Moreover, the medical profession itself would have a vested interest in minimizing price or quality competition. In any case, doctors or hospitals would frequently enjoy local monopolies because of geographical factors. Only large urban areas would be able to support more than one hospital and, even then, there might be only one hospital specializing in many of the rarer conditions. More seriously, as the recent development of private hospitals in Britain has shown, the pattern of provision would depend on profitability rather than need – with ample choice for relatively low-cost operations and considerably less for 'Cinderella services' such as geriatric care.

Similarly, will the privatization of British Telecom lead to extra choice for the ordinary householder – other than at the trivial level of Mickey Mouse sets rather than Trimphones? It is difficult to see how the domestic user can be offered the choice of alternative lines to each house. In fact, it is the more lucrative business-user market which is the real attraction for private-sector producers. And here the danger is that a public-sector monopoly will, by and large, simply be replaced by a private-sector monopoly. Fears are already being expressed about the possibility of this happening in an industry so basically involved

9. Galbraith, op. cit., p. 220.

in the emerging 'information revolution'. United States experience, for example, suggests that the need will soon arise for state regulation of private-sector activities in such an area – thereby imposing a straitjacket of control in place of the de-control that is the purported essence of privatization.

If width of consumer choice is limited within the private sector, it is not obvious either that privatization would automatically lead to better *quality* of products or provision of services. There is an abundance of examples of the wastes of competition – duplication of facilities (for example, petrol stations), the burden of selling costs (advertising and unnecessary packaging) and built-in obsolescence – or its failure adequately to satisfy consumer wants (for instance, car servicing and repair). A transfer of production from the public sector to the private sector is not necessarily a guarantee either of increased competition or of a resultant improvement in the quality of output.

At a time when energetic attempts are being made to reduce the public sector, it is worth recalling the arguments behind the increased public output of goods and services that has taken place over the years. Thus in some areas, such as national defence or law enforcement, we must either consume a service collectively or not at all: it is simply not on to have private-sector soldiers or prisons. Similarly it would be impossible to provide a complete road system in the private sector. With other goods and services, there is a grave danger that, if left to private-sector provision, too little would be consumed. In health and education, for instance, poorer or less caring consumers would be tempted to economize. The effects would be felt, partly by their dependants but also by the rest of society as the productivity of less fit and less educated workers impaired our national output. Our economic interdependence means that illiteracy and ill-health can drag down the standard of living of all the population. And anyway it is frequently not a matter of public versus private output but, because of their interdependence, of how to secure an appropriate *balance* between them.

Take, for example, the obvious case of private versus public transport. To own your own car gives you privacy, flexibility and the freedom of the roads. In contrast, public transport is often irregular, inflexible, overcrowded, slow and more expensive. But the basis of comparison is hardly a fair one. After all, *why* are urban bus services slow, infrequent and relatively expensive? Because of the congestion caused by private cars extravagant of road-space, because increased car ownership has reduced the demand for bus services and forced up their price. Given the resulting inadequacies of public transport there is every inducement for still more people to use their cars for the journey to work – to the consequent detriment of *both* other car users and those still travelling by bus. We are caught in a vicious circle. And the choice between private and public transport should be presented not in terms as they are now, but as alternative combinations of the two as they *could* be. If, for example, the car was banned from city centres, the quality and extent of public services which could then be provided would certainly be very different from what they currently offer.

Transport also provides an illustration of one of the more absurd, if not most serious, flaws in the present composition of output. The system fails to produce even those public goods necessary for the enjoyment of the private consumption to which the economy is primarily geared. An increase in the number of car owners requires an expansion of the road system. But road-building and town-planning have not kept pace – with the familiar results of urban snarl-ups, frustration, high accident rates and pollution. American experience suggests that the answer may not lie in bigger and better roads, because they merely increase car use still further and perpetuate the problem on a larger scale. We might therefore have to tackle the problem the other way round – by limiting car use to the capacity of the available roads. Striking the right balance is no easy matter. The important thing is that we should be able to see clearly what are the different packages of private and public consumption between which we have to choose. Generally at the present time these are not made clear.

Other arguments for increased collective consumption are those connected with the general quality of life and the need for public goods and services to be produced on a substantial scale if maximum enjoyment is to be derived from private consumption. Increasing lip-service is paid to the importance of enhancing the environment in which we live. Yet this will not happen through the workings of the market. Increasingly, as we grow richer, we shall require outlets for the constructive enjoyment of our leisure. Yet the fisherman today finds his sport ruined by polluted rivers, the family motorist sometimes reduced to picnicking in a litter-strewn layby. Cleaning up the mess already caused to the environment, providing the required range of leisure activities, including continued education, and generally creating conditions in which people find it pleasant to live will all require a shift to more collective consumption if the Galbraithian nightmare of 'private affluence, public squalor' is to be avoided.

There is no doubt that public-sector spending is viewed with suspicion by many people and there are a number of reasons for this. In the first place, in assessing our standard of living, how well-off we are, most of us tend to concentrate on the amount of private consumption which we can manage to undertake. We generally fail to include as part of our total material welfare the benefits we derive from the range of public services which are provided – health, education, libraries, parks and so on. Awareness of the importance of these services is one of the reasons why American visitors to Britain sometimes used to argue with disbelieving natives that the U.K. standard of living was higher than their own.

A further bias against collective consumption arises from the fact that we do not all benefit equally from the provision of public services. We all help to pay for the building of inter-city motorways but the beneficiaries are the car-owners who use them. The childless still have to contribute towards the cost of schools. The healthy help to finance the treatment of the chronically sick. In other words, we do not always see any very direct link between what we pay and what we get back.

Moreover, while considerable resources are poured into sectors like higher education, which, on ample evidence, is still largely enjoyed by children of middle-class parentage, other services which benefit much larger numbers are often relatively neglected. Replacement of antiquated school buildings in urban slums, the provision of parks, adventure playgrounds and low-cost housing lag behind partly because those who would benefit from them are less organized and vocal.

Then again there is the problem of financing public consumption. There is a deep-rooted prejudice against paying taxes. It is astonishing how many people remain convinced that taxes are largely frittered away in governmental extravagance and fail to connect them at all with the range of real benefits which they help to finance. This reluctance to see the 'burden of taxation' increased is, of course, fostered and reinforced by the whole ethos of the industrial system, which continually extols the virtues of more and more private consumption.

And the recent argument that privatization 'reduces the burden on the public purse' does not bear close scrutiny. If anything, it is likely to add to the need for taxation since the only industries that can be privatized are those already making profits, part of which might have accrued to the State. Financially, privatization does help to hold down the P.S.B.R. – with the sale once and for all of public assets obviating the need for that amount of borrowing. We have already questioned the relevance of the P.S.B.R. as an indication of government economic prudence; and if advocates of the 'crowding-out' hypothesis *were* correct, then would not the sale of industries at present publicly owned have a similarly deleterious effect on new private-sector investment?

A further reason for our reluctance to support public-sector activity is that, because parts of the public sector show little or no profit, they are deemed to be less efficient than the private sector. It is often argued, for instance, that because British Rail struggles every year to balance its books, this clearly indicates less efficiency than if it were subject to the simple yardstick of private profit. What this neglects, however, are potentially important 'external' costs and benefits that do not appear in a private company's balance-sheet.

What has to be made clear is that 'commercial' is not to be equated with 'economic'. And, secondly, that there is no need for us to resign ourselves to the view that what is 'economic' is necessarily desirable, and that the 'non-economic' must always be rejected out of hand.

Because production is commercially viable – the revenue resulting from it exceeding the costs which firms have incurred – it does not always follow that it is economic. Nor do financial losses for a company necessarily indicate that it has been engaged in production which was uneconomic. Whether or not output is economic depends not just on the extent the companies concerned are doing well or badly, but on the net effect of their activities on the community as a whole. The difference between the economic as opposed to the commercial criterion is that it takes into account external or 'spillover' effects.

Thus the factory that belches smoke into the surrounding neighbourhood or dumps its effluent into an adjoining river creates costs in the process. But they are not costs which will appear in its own balance sheet. They are costs which are borne by others – the housewife coping with the family washing, the bronchial patients in the doctor's waiting room, the local authority using the river as a source of drinking water and those who previously used the river for a variety of pleasurable activities. Similarly commercial airlines currently making profits would certainly not do so if they had to compensate those who bear the cost of aircraft noise in the districts surrounding major airports. Or take the matter of industrial location. The firm that sets up business in an area of already concentrated industrial activity does so because that is what is suggested by its estimates of private costs and yields. It is the community which carries the costs of straining resources and amenities which are already working near full capacity. If that firm could only be induced to move to a development area, not only would these additional social costs be avoided but positive benefits might result. The value of time wasted by every other road user does not show in the costing of a particular firm whose lorries add to an existing congestion problem; nor does the saving in unemployment benefit appear as part of the profit of a firm hiring labour in a development area. What makes sense for the economy as a whole may not seem so to the individual companies involved.

Private firms are concerned only with output which it *pays* them to produce. What it is economic to produce, on the other hand, can be decided only when wider spillover effects, both costs and benefits, are taken into account. But that should still not be the end of the matter – although it often is. Such is the sway which economics today has on our thinking that for a particular project to be labelled 'non-economic' is a clear indication that it should be consigned to the wastepaper basket. But are there no circumstances in which we think *non*-economic aspects important enough to outweigh purely economic considerations? Are we only interested in devoting resources to education, for example, if there are clear economic gains from doing so?

Ideally, then, the composition of output would be determined not on a commercial basis dictated by profit maximization, but in such a way that spillover effects are fully taken into account and the production which takes place is that which maximizes the *social surplus* of benefits over costs. In principle this can be calculated by the use of cost-benefit analysis.

A well-known early application of cost-benefit techniques was the study by C. D. Foster and M. Beesley of the economics of the Victoria Line extension to the London Underground railway system.[10] On a commercial basis, there seemed little prospect of the line paying its way. On the contrary, it was predicted that it would have an annual operating loss of about £2 million, with an additional loss of £1 million to the underground system as a whole as passengers took advantage of the shorter routes provided by the new line. However, Foster and Beesley tried to estimate the wider social benefits which would

10. C. D. Foster and M. E. Beesley, 'Estimating the Social Benefit of Constructing an Underground Railway in London', *Journal of the Royal Statistical Society*, 1963.

arise from the construction of the Victoria Line – for example, the time-savings both of those using the Victoria Line and those road-users now facing less congestion as a result of some surface-travellers now preferring to go by underground. They concluded that the economic as opposed to commercial return on the line might be in the order of 11 per cent.

Cost-benefit analysis offers the attractive possibility of establishing whether a project will be beneficial to society as a whole rather than just the individual enterprise involved in it. But cost-benefit analysis does not provide any objective, scientific answers. Its use for ranking projects in order of priority depends entirely on the values which are injected into analysis. For example, two of the external costs involved in the siting of a new international airport would certainly be the noise nuisance to local residents and passenger inconvenience caused by a particular situation. But quite apart from problems of measuring them, there is the further question of the relative *weights* which should be attached to the two costs. If, again, the benefits of a project exceed the costs but the benefits largely accrue to a minority of rich individuals while the costs are mostly borne by a majority of poorer people, should the project still be undertaken? We can either value costs and benefits at present market prices (which reflect the present distribution of income) and accept that a pound's worth of benefit or cost has the same value regardless of who gains or loses – which is an implicit acceptance of the principles underlying the status quo – or we can use 'shadow prices' reflecting a more optimal income distribution, and make deliberate judgements that certain classes of cost and benefit should count more heavily than others. In this case, we are talking about what *ought* to be. The virtue of cost-benefit analysis is that it forces decision-makers to take an explicit stand on relative social values.

To show that a particular project will generate benefits in excess of costs does not necessarily mean that it should therefore be undertaken. Such a decision should be made only after the project has been compared with others, some of which may show a greater social surplus. But often cost-benefit analysis has been used to justify a particular investment without any attempt to put it in a ranking order with alternative schemes.

Use of cost-benefit analysis is particularly attractive for government departments, partly because it offers the possibility of measuring non-marketed services, and partly because the public sector accepts wider responsibilities than the purely commercial. But from the point of view of achieving a more acceptable composition of output, clearly the principle of taking into account social costs and benefits must be extended throughout the economy as a whole. If private enterprises operate on an exclusively commercial basis, serious divergencies between private and social gains and losses may emerge. But are firms still only profit-maximizers or have they already themselves begun to assume wider responsibilities? Should they be subject to 'social-efficiency audits' by a government body charged with ensuring that private and social objectives are kept broadly in line?

That is not the current mood. On the contrary, recent moves towards purely commercial privatization have been accepted by the public at large with some enthusiasm and surprisingly little resistance. One of the reasons for this must be a degree of disillusionment with the public sector as it has operated.

Thus nationalized industries are widely regarded as an inefficient, loss-making, troublesome drain – an additional financial cross for the taxpayer to bear. For many such industries this is simply untrue. More generally there is little understanding of what the *objectives* of public industries ought properly to be. This confusion has been compounded over the years by governments that have *used* nationalized industries in a variety of ways which have not been conducive to their future development; as 'residuary legatees' of investment funds to compensate for the vagaries of the private sector, as counter-inflationary weapons with prices being held to artificially low levels, as milch-cows with prices raised to provide concealed tax increases.

But there is one important respect in which both nationalized industries and the state provision of public services must certainly be regarded as having failed. Both are all too commonly viewed by the consuming public as bureaucratic, inaccessible and unresponsive to their wants and needs. And for the workers in such industries, there has been little success in breaking down 'them and us' attitudes that might have been expected in publicly rather than privately operated enterprises. It is on these shortcomings – the failure to create a sense of involvement among consumers and workers in their 'own' enterprises, the lack of *socialization* of public-sector activity – that critics of privatization would be advised to ponder.

The emotive appeal of 'freeing' the economy by 'getting the State off our backs' probably has greatest attraction for an age-group (now in the majority) who cannot recall pre-Welfare State society. 'Freedom to choose' has a resounding rhetoric until it is recognized that the freedom may be limited to the relatively few.

The major argument for state rather than private provision of a wide variety of goods and services is, to return to Enoch Powell's analogy with which we opened this chapter, that in fact we live in a profoundly *un*democratic economic system when voting power is highly unequally distributed. All consumers may be enfranchised, but some to a far greater extent than others.

It is within the framework of such inequalities that the pattern of output is determined. The sources of inequality in the distribution of income and wealth, and their effects, are therefore of such significance as to warrant our attention in the next two chapters.

12

Fair Pay?

The last three chapters have concentrated on consumers and producers and the relationship between them in the 'final goods market', where finished products and services are bought and sold. We have questioned just how efficiently the private sector supplies goods and services to consumers and whether economic efficiency would indeed improve if the private sector took over the production of some goods and services at present provided by the State.

But in addition to the final goods market there is also a set of 'factor markets' in which buyers and sellers of resources – land, labour and capital – are brought together. With what result? What determines the price of a factor of production like labour? What light does economics shed on the distribution of income between individuals and classes? In this chapter we shall concentrate on the question of the distribution of income from *work*. Why do doctors earn more than dustmen, managing directors more than miners? And can differentials as wide as those which we have be economically and morally justified?

The real world is one of enormously complex and often very extreme disparities in incomes. We will therefore approach it cautiously, first of all blandly assuming away all its complications and then re-introducing them one at a time.

Begin by imagining an economy in which three conditions hold good: (i) that perfect competition exists throughout; buyers and sellers of both final goods and factors of production like labour are all too small independently to influence the price of whatever it is that they are buying and selling; (ii) that labour is homogeneous – all workers are quite identical, both physically and mentally; (iii) that factors of production, including labour, are perfectly mobile between jobs and areas. Obviously these are all highly unrealistic assumptions. But if they did hold good, what prediction could we make about the distribution of income earned from work?

In such an extraordinary economy, incomes from work would be broadly equalized. Firms would hire workers to the point at which the extra wage they had to pay out was just covered by the extra revenue which they earned from the consequent increase in sales. In economists' jargon, wages would be equal to the marginal productivity of labour. But this would tend to be the same in all industries. Suppose that temporarily this were not so and that wages and marginal productivity in the car industry, for example, rose above those in coal-mining. The result would be that miners would leave the coalfields and move into the car-producing areas; the increased supply of labour would force down car workers' wages. Meanwhile the reduction in workforce would be pushing up wages in the mining industry. Free movement of homogeneous factors in a perfect market works to eliminate income differentials. And wages, like the price of anything else, are determined by demand and supply.

But not entirely. For, although we have assumed that workers are all identical, the jobs they do will still be very different. Some will be interesting, others dull; some in warm, congenial conditions, others dirty and dangerous. Therefore what will be equalized in this imaginary situation are not incomes, but *net advantages*. The net advantages of a job include not just what it pays but also its non-pecuniary aspects. What we might expect is that dustmen would receive rather higher wages than those in occupations which in themselves are more rewarding and satisfying – like, for example, university professors. The differential in earnings between the two jobs would depend on how much extra cash university professors needed to induce them to give up their comfortable chairs and take to the cold streets.

It is time to drop the absurd assumptions with which we

started. For the major explanation of the wide disparities in income from work in the real world is that these conditions do *not* hold good. There is not perfect competition, labour is not homogeneous, and it is not perfectly mobile.

For a start, then, part of the wage differentials between groups of workers results from monopolistic bargaining by trade unions able, through the closed shop and other restrictions, to limit the supply of labour and keep its price artificially high. Differentials arise because workers are not all organized to the same extent and because bargaining power varies from industry to industry. However, although these 'imperfections' of the labour market certainly help to explain the difference in wage rates between, say, car workers in Oxford and textile workers in Blackburn, they are by no means the most important of the factors making for unequal distribution of income from work.

The second assumption to be dropped is that of homogeneity of labour. Workers differ from each other first of all because of an unequal dispersion of 'natural talent'. This term is used in the very broadest sense. To begin with, we come in very different shapes and sizes: some are physically strong, others dexterous, others again feeble or disabled. Beyond these, there are differences in other faculties. Some people are more intelligent, some have musical gifts which others lack, some have drive and verve, others are naturally slow or indolent. How far these qualities are inborn and how much they are due to environmental influences is a fascinating and important question which is beyond our present scope. The fact is, whether we like it or not, by the time a child begins school, marked differences in ability, temperament and motivation are already deeply rooted and more likely to be reinforced rather than reduced by formal education.

What are the economic implications? Some talents, like physical strength, are likely to be in abundant supply. Others, like the ability to play violin concertos, will be confined to a few. Those who possess a talent in short supply for which there is a positive demand will be able to earn what economists have termed a 'rent of ability'.

This concept – of economic rent – needs a little explanation. It has nothing directly to do with the rent which is paid for houses, but is defined as a payment to a factor in scarce supply over and above its transfer earnings. Take the case for example of a pop singer who before being discovered was working as a bricklayer. Let's also suppose that the only other job he could do, apart from singing, *is* bricklaying – at which he could make £130 a week. Then this £130 is known as his transfer earnings – it is the amount which he could earn in his next-best occupation. Therefore, all that we have to pay him to continue to sing is marginally above £130. If in fact he earns tens of thousands a week, then all of that above £130 is economic rent. It is a payment to him over and above what is needed to keep him in his present occupation.

The reason why pop singers, film stars, footballers and the like often earn vast sums is twofold. Firstly, they have 'talents' which are in extremely scarce supply and cannot easily be increased. And, secondly, there is a demand for those talents. Just having a rare ability – to be able to wiggle one's ears, for example – does not guarantee high rent earnings. The amount of rent depends entirely on the *demand* for the scarce ability.

The concept of economic rent not only throws some light on exotic income disparities like these; it also helps to understand more mundane wage differentials. Suppose, for example, that private cars are banned from a city centre. This will mean that a great deal more public transport will have to be provided. More bus drivers will be needed and one way of attracting them will be to increase wages from, say, £90 a week to £100 a week. The £100 will have to be paid, of course, not just to the new recruits but also to the drivers who previously worked for the bus company. For *them*, the extra £10 is a rent element in their earnings. It is more than necessary to keep them bus-driving – because before they had been prepared to accept only £90 a week. In this case, however, the £10 is termed 'quasi-rent', being really only a short-term bonus arising from a temporary shortage of a particular skill which can be fairly easily increased in the long run.

As well as differences in 'natural ability' in the workforce, there are those which result from education and training. A great deal more time and money has been spent on preparing a doctor for his vocation than on a dustman. In terms of economic analysis, this can be seen as *investment* in human capital – investment in the sense that resources have been used in education and training which could otherwise have been currently consumed. The result is that there is no such thing as 'pure labour'. Nuclear physicists are highly 'capital-intensive', embodying a great deal of investment; others, like postmen, are much more 'labour-intensive' workers, with little training. And in economics, the return to capital is interest. Part of the differential between workers of different skills is therefore to be explained by the fact that earnings include an element of interest in addition to pure wages.

Finally, what is the effect of discarding the third assumption of our initial model – that labour is perfectly mobile? In the real world, free movement of workers is limited in a number of ways. Firstly, between areas: workers may be reluctant to move to more prosperous regions because of a host of uncertainties, expense and unwillingness to be uprooted. Secondly, between jobs of a similar kind within the same area: the level of skill required in coal-mining and engineering may be roughly the same, for example, but it may not be easy for the redundant coal-miner to acquire the new engineering skills which would create an employment opportunity for him. Thirdly, and most restricted of all, is movement between different *classes* of job: social immobility. It may be possible for the doctor to become a dustman but the reverse is certainly quite out of the question. Of course, the dustman's *son* could become a doctor, but even his chances of doing so are generally much worse than those of the *doctor's* son. Certainly social mobility in Britain has increased considerably over recent decades, but it is still very limited. The continued existence of private education and the cumulative effects of initial income, wealth and environmental disparities combine to restrict entry into many professions to a tiny minority of the working population.

The effect of imperfect immobility is that there is not a single market for labour in the economy; instead it is fragmented into a large number of non-competing groups. *Within* each of these groups, earnings for similar sorts of work will be roughly brought into line by the forces of supply and demand and movement between jobs. Thus a rise in car workers' wages in Oxford will have some effect on the incomes of other semi-skilled labour in the area. What happens is that when the car industry is expanding and taking on more workers, shortages develop in the supply, for example, of painters and decorators, who, if the demand for their services remains unchanged, will be able to push up the prices which they charge to their customers. But *between* groups, on the other hand, economic forces will have little equalizing effect because of lack of movement between them. An increase in the salaries paid to university professors, for instance, will have no effect whatever on the wages paid to car workers.

It is at this point that we can begin to see the limitations of traditional economics in providing an adequate account of the differences in earnings from work. It does seem genuinely useful as providing an analytical framework within which differentials of various sorts can be categorized; we can see that disparities arise because of differential bargaining power, because of uneven dispersion of abilities and aptitudes, because of differences in education and training and because of highly imperfect mobility of labour. Earnings from work can be seen as an amalgam of pure wages, monopolistic surpluses, interest on investment in human capital and various elements of economic rent.

But what the theory does not really offer is an explanation of these differentials. Take, in particular, the gap between the earnings of non-competing groups. Traditional theory takes us only to the point of recognizing that one of the reasons for differentials between professional and manual workers is that there is practically no upward mobility between the two groups. But what decides the extent of the disparity between them? Why does one group earn, say, ten times as much as the other, rather than five times as much? On this question economics has little to say.

In fact such differentials are a reflection of our social valuations: they express what we think one group of workers *ought* to earn in comparison with others. Doctors get paid a great deal more than dustmen because, as a society, we 'value' their services more highly. Managing directors can command salaries fantastically in excess of earnings on the shop floor because, as a society, we have come to accept that this is right and proper. Film stars and the like earn the enormous sums they do because, as a society, we agree that scarce talents deserve high rewards.

These are the values which underlie our present extremely unequal distribution of income from work. They are seldom expressly articulated, but they are nonetheless an implicit element in the process of wage bargaining and salary determination.

It is time that they were made explicit. They *may* be valuations which the majority of people find perfectly defensible and acceptable. On the other hand, once they were exposed, the principles on which incomes are distributed might seem to many to be profoundly unfair. The important thing is that they should be brought into the open for discussion by everyone rather than just the economic cognoscenti. Such a debate has hardly yet begun despite the fact that the issues involved are basic to the solution of many of our present economic problems.

We have to examine both the economic necessity and the moral justifiability of inequality. Perhaps widely unequal incomes are a vital element in the efficient functioning of the economic system but are morally unjust. Perhaps they are both economically necessary *and* morally acceptable. And perhaps they are neither. It is to these real issues that we now turn.

Is Inequality Economically Necessary?

There are a number of grounds on which it can be argued that inequality is essential if the economy is to run as we want it to. The first of these concerns the relationship between income distribution, savings and economic growth.

The poor are not known for their thriftiness; indeed if they are very poor the whole of their income has to be used up in providing for their immediate needs. Generally speaking, the more an individual earns, the greater the amount he is able and willing to save. Some go further than this and suggest (although the evidence is by no means clear) that high-income groups save not only a larger absolute amount than low-income groups, but also a greater *proportion* of their income. Therefore the greater the inequality in the distribution of income, the larger the volume of savings which an economy is likely to generate. For society, these savings allow an accumulation of capital – stored-up production which has not been frittered away in current consumption. It enables more investment to take place in factories, machines and all the other factors needed for greater production in the future. More equality therefore means less saving, less economic growth. We can have more consumption today, but only at the price of less jam tomorrow.

Secondly, there is the matter of incentives. It is argued that, human nature being what it is, a hierarchical distribution of incomes makes people wish to better themselves – to rise up the income strata and emulate those above them whom they envy. Take away differentials and the incentive to work harder is lost. Once again, the effect will be a fall in output. Moreover, removal of differentials between jobs and regions will remove the inducement for workers to move from one job and area to another. The economy will become fossilized in a rigid pattern of production and lack the flexibility which is called for by rapidly changing technology. And how, in an egalitarian society, can people be persuaded to undertake those jobs which are dirty, dangerous or particularly demanding in other ways? Would, for example, young people be prepared to undertake the long hard sacrificial slog of high school, university and post-graduate training unless they knew that at the end of the road they would be rewarded for their efforts by being paid substantially more than those who opted out at an earlier stage?

One way of testing the strength of these arguments for inequality is to suppose that in this country, for example, a law was passed so that overnight incomes became broadly equalized. What would happen to the economy?

Taking the growth point first, whether the amount of personal savings would be reduced depends on a number of factors. Those whose incomes fell to the new average would save less. But those whose incomes rose would save more. Only if it is true that the rich save a greater *proportion* of their income than the poor would the fact that some now save less offset the greater saving which would be undertaken by others. Then again, many savings institutions which are now geared to the requirements of their richer clients would be forced to adapt to the new situation and devise schemes which would help to increase the propensity to save of the now average lower-income groups. Moreover, a further potential source of savings would be opened up by the elimination of the conspicuous consumption of the rich which the present highly unequal distribution of income and wealth makes possible. It was Keynes, after all, who said that during the nineteenth century 'capitalists were allowed the greater part of the national cake on condition that they didn't eat it', and it is doubtful whether that condition – that high personal incomes are heavily ploughed back into productive investment – holds good to anything like the same extent today. And, finally, the greater part of saving in a modern economy is not in fact done by individuals anyway; it is the province of firms and the State itself. If therefore the amount of personal saving in a more egalitarian economy turned out to be insufficient, the authorities could either encourage more institutional saving or do the job themselves through taxation. In any case, it can be argued that the volume of saving is only a contributory element in the growth process, and that economic growth should not be an aim *per se*. On this argument, 'losses' under this heading (if indeed there were any as a result of equal income distribution) should perhaps not be taken too seriously.

And what of the argument that without income differentials

there would be a major weakening of incentives to work, to move and to accept jobs which are particularly demanding? This is really very suspect. Would the managing director, since he was now being paid no more than any other worker, say, 'There's no longer any point in worrying myself with the power and responsibility of running this firm' – and go down and join them on the shop floor? Would school leavers really opt to go straight into industry at sixteen rather than suffer the rigours of further education once they realized that they were not going to command much higher incomes as a reward for their prolonged studies? Doubtless there would be cases like this. But not many, because in fact we do jobs, not just for the money involved, but because they happen to satisfy other personal urges (or, more sadly, because we lack the gifts to do the things that we would really like to do). Responsible posts would still be filled, because there are many people who *enjoy* taking decisions and holding positions of power. And even dirty and dangerous jobs would still be manned either by those who for some personal reason prefer them, or by those who are unable to find pleasanter or safer employment. An egalitarian world would not, unfortunately, automatically guarantee everyone the job opportunity of his first choice. But it would at least be one in which the reluctant dustman has the consolation of knowing that he is being paid as much as the professional man who has a more varied and comfortable position. And to a large extent, after all, one might expect the number of dirty and dangerous jobs to be reduced once incomes were more equally distributed. It is because many occupations have traditionally been low-paid that they have also become unpleasant; low pay has retarded mechanization which could remove some of the more disagreeable aspects of the work.

All in all, then, there are no clearly compelling economic reasons for income differentials, except perhaps to equalize the 'net advantages' of various jobs along the lines we discussed earlier. And this would be a distribution markedly different from the present one, in that the dustman might well expect to receive a rather higher return than the doctor.

Is Inequality Morally Justifiable?

The moral case for inequality is even more tenuous. As we have seen, economics can be used to identify four sources of income disparities: variations in bargaining strength of working groups; uneven spread of abilities; differences in education and training; and imperfect mobility.

But those differentials which stem from the greater power of some groups over others – whether it is because they are better organized, or occupy a peculiarly strategic position in the economy, or are able effectively to determine their own incomes as managers do – are not obviously deserving of moral approbation. Then again, to be born clever or musical or physically strong is nothing but a matter of chance; it seems a somewhat odd morality which highly rewards those who have been lucky, while saying to the unintelligent, the tone-deaf and the physically disabled: 'Not only have you had the misfortune to be born with these handicaps. We will continue to penalize you for them for the rest of your life by employing you in uninteresting, unpleasant, ill-paid jobs.' (And the 'economic rent' payments to the talented are clearly not *necessary*, since by definition they are over and above what is required to keep people in their present occupations.)

Nor is the education/training justification for inequalities very convincing – the argument that those who have been prepared to make the sacrifice involved then deserve higher earnings analogous to interest payable on capital. Take the case of undergraduates, for example. In the first place, much of what they do at university should be classified as consumption rather than investment; they are there, not just because of their future prospects, but also because they enjoy being at college. Secondly, how far are they really making any 'sacrifice'? Certainly they have forfeited the earnings which they could have made between the age when they could have left school and the time when they become graduates. But these are likely to be minimal, given the fact that they would have lacked any significant qualifications. Moreover, during their time at university these losses are anyway partially offset by state grants and earnings from vacation jobs. And yet for the lucky ones who these days find graduate occupations, a university degree is still a passport to a lifetime of substantially higher incomes than the non-graduate is likely to earn.

To the extent that higher education *is* a genuine 'investment' and involves the use of resources (buildings, equipment and teachers) which could otherwise have been used for present consumption, who has made the necessary sacrifice? It is seldom the students themselves. Either it is their own parents who bear the cost, or it is the general taxpayer. If therefore it is right that interest should be paid on the capital tied up in higher education, it is parents and taxpayers who should receive it rather than the fortunate beneficiaries of extended education.

And, finally, what moral justification can there possibly be for the differentials (largely unexplained by economics) between the various non-competing groups in the economy? These disparities, as we have seen, come about chiefly because of the impediments in the way of movement between different classes of jobs. And such obstacles become cumulative in an economic system in which wealth can be handed down from generation to generation. It is here that those who advocate 'equality of opportunity' as the key to a fairer society miss the point that income inequalities will continue to widen so long as the starting point is one between initial unequals. Suppose, for example, that not only do we establish equal incomes throughout the economy but simultaneously abolish public schools and other manifestations of a socially divided system. All children will now be from homes with the same family income and attend exactly the same sort of schools. But who will benefit most? It will still tend to be the children of middle-class parents – from a home background in which learning is given priority, in which books and study facilities are made freely available. *Full* social equality means in the first place positive discrimination in favour of those who start with an initial handicap. Our own system, on the other hand, works on precisely the opposite lines, granting cumulative advantages to those who begin from a more favoured position.

To sum up, the practical outcome of the market with regard to income distribution is likely to be highly inegalitarian, with the gap between rich and poor tending to widen rather than diminish. Yet, on examination, there are no compelling economic reasons for income inequalities; and the social norms which lie behind market forces, when made explicit, embody an extremely dubious morality. If this is so, how can inequalities on the scale which exist in our own economy possibly be justified? How great they are and the fundamental problems which stem from them are the subjects of the next chapter.

13

The National Wealth

So much for the theory of distribution. Traditional economics provides a means of categorizing income differentials but does little to explain or justify them. And the case for inequality – in both practice and principle – turns out, on inspection, to be a very weak one. But just what are the facts of the matter? How much inequality is there in a modern industrial economy such as Britain's? In this chapter we look at the degree of inequality – in personal incomes, and in the share-out of national wealth.

First of all, then, the way in which incomes are distributed between individuals. Starting at the apex of the income pyramid, the top 1 per cent of income earners in this country, in 1978–9, took 5·2 per cent of total pre-tax incomes (rather less, incidentally, than they manage to cream off in the United States or most underdeveloped countries). The top 10 per cent have 24·2 per cent of total incomes. And when we switch our attention to the other end of the scale, we find that the poorest 20 per cent of income earners have got only 9 per cent of the national income (and that, by the way, is a higher proportion than the 5 per cent which is the commonly quoted figure for the United States). Broadly, this is a distribution pattern found in most advanced capitalist countries – with some, such as Germany or France, rather more unequal, and others, such as Sweden or Israel, rather less so.

There is no more brilliantly vivid account of what those rather dry statistics mean in personal terms than that of Jan Pen,[1] who portrays a Grand Parade lasting just one hour during

1. J. Pen, *Income Distribution*, Allen Lane The Penguin Press, 1971.

which the whole of the British population march past in ascending order of height, their heights corresponding to the levels of their incomes. We, the spectators, are assumed to be of average height (that is, we earn the average income for the economy as a whole). Pen describes the dramatic unfolding of the spectacle as we see it from our vantage point.

'We see tiny gnomes pass by, the size of a matchstick, a cigarette ... housewives who have worked for a short time and so have got nothing like an annual income, schoolboys with a paper round ... It takes perhaps five minutes for them to pass.' The next five or six minutes sees 'an increase by leaps and bounds. The people still passing by are still very small ones – about three feet – but they are noticeably taller than their predecessors ... They include some young people ... very many old-age pensioners ... divorced women ... owners of shops doing poor trade ... unemployed persons.' Next 'the ordinary workers about whom there is nothing out of the ordinary except that they are in the lowest-paid jobs. Dustmen, Underground ticket collectors, some miners. The unskilled clerks march in front of the unskilled manual workers ... We also see a large number of coloured persons ... It takes almost fifteen minutes before the passing marchers reach a height of substantially more than four feet. For you and me this is a disturbing sight; fifteen minutes is a long time to keep seeing small people pass who barely reach to our midriff.'

Nor, as this group finally passes, is there any immediate relief from this macabre spectacle. Instead, 'we keep seeing dwarfs ... After another ten minutes small people approach who reach to our collar bones. We see skilled industrial workers, people with considerable training. Office workers, respectable persons, so to say. We know that the parade will last an hour and perhaps we expected that after half-an-hour we would be able to look the marchers straight in the eye, but that is not so. We are still looking down on the top of their heads, and even in the distance we do not yet see any obvious improvement. The height is growing with tantalizing slowness, and *forty-five*

minutes have gone by before we see people of our own size arriving'
(italics added).

These are teachers, executive civil servants, clerical workers, shopkeepers, insurance agents, foremen, a few farmers. But it is the last six minutes of the parade which becomes sensational with the arrival of the top 10 per cent.

Modestly tall to begin with (about six feet six inches): headmasters, youngish university graduates, seamen, farmers, departmental heads. 'They are people who had never thought that they belonged to the top 10 per cent.'

And then the climax packed into the last few minutes. 'Giants suddenly loom up. A lawyer, not exceptionally successful: eighteen feet tall ... The first doctors come into sight, seven or eight yards, the first accountants. There is still one minute to go, and now we see towering fellows. University professors, nine yards, senior officers of large concerns, ten yards, a Permanent Secretary thirteen yards tall, and an even taller High Court judge; a few accountants, eye surgeons and surgeons of twenty yards or more.'

'During the last seconds the scene is dominated by colossal figures people like tower blocks. Most of them prove to be businessmen, managers of large firms and holders of many directorships, and also film stars and a few members of the Royal Family ... Prince Philip, sixty yards ... Tom Jones: nearly a mile high ... John Paul Getty. His height is inconceivable: at least ten miles, and perhaps twice as much.'

What is disturbing about these figures, in view of the arguments of the previous chapter, is not just the concentration of income at the very top of the scale – the continued existence of the super-rich. It is the extent of the disparities which exist lower down the scale – between more ordinary mortals like the average worker and the average manager. And in this respect, Britain is perhaps somewhat exceptional amongst otherwise comparable economies. Why should it be necessary in this country that the ratio between their incomes should be much wider than it is, for example, in Japan?

It can be argued that the picture of massive inequalities which has emerged so far is exaggerated because the incomes which we have been comparing are *pre*-tax. With a taxation system which is progressive – taking a greater *proportion* of richer people's incomes – inequality should appear much less if we compare *post-tax* incomes. However, evidence suggests that inequality is only slightly reduced by the workings of the tax system. First, this is because the British tax system is anyway only partly progressive; in addition to income taxes, there are indirect taxes falling on rich and poor consumers alike simply according to what they buy – and indirect taxes form a substantial proportion of total government revenue. Secondly, higher-income groups tend on the whole to find the process of tax avoidance a great deal easier than those lower down the income scale; the professional financial and accounting journals are full of advertisements offering a whole range of methods for reducing tax burdens. And, thirdly, there is the problem of defining precisely what should be included in the concept of income itself; higher income groups tend to enjoy not only larger monetary rewards, but also a much greater range of fringe benefits.

There is no doubt about two facts: that there has been a marked change in the distribution since before the war, but that income is still very unequally distributed in Britain today. Most of the narrowing of inequality which has taken place was between 1938 and 1949. Calculations suggest, for example, that the share of income going to the top 1 per cent fell sharply from 17·1 per cent in 1938–9 to 10·6 per cent in 1949–50; the top 5 per cent received 31·5 per cent of total income in 1938–9 and 23·1 per cent in 1949–50; meanwhile, at the other end of the scale, the share of income going to the lowest 30 per cent of income earners remained constant at 13·8 per cent.[2] This represented a major redistribution, although its extent may be exaggerated by the fact that the top group increasingly took their incomes in forms which the figures conceal.[3]

2. Royal Commission on Income and Wealth Report No 1, Cmnd 6171.

3. R. M. Titmuss, *Income Distribution and Social Change*, Allen & Unwin, 1962.

The process of redistribution has subsequently continued at a much slower and more halting pace – with, for example, the share of the top 10 per cent of income-earners reduced from 33·2 per cent in 1949 to 24·8 per cent in 1979–80.[4] But there have been pointers that at times the poor may have become relatively poorer. This is partly because the middle-income groups tend to use social services – for example, higher education – much more extensively than those in the lower-income strata; partly because they are able to capitalize on tax concessions to a greater extent (a classic example is the extent to which those fortunate enough to own their houses have their mortgage interest subsidized); and partly because there have sometimes been substantial increases in a number of regressive taxes – increases in local authority rents and rates, in national insurance and health contributions – coupled with withdrawals of subsidies on, for instance, food and school milk.

The mass of people in this country have never been better off than they are today, as can be judged by the extent to which the average family owns consumer durables like cars, radio and television and washing machines. Affluence today is more dispersed than ever before – and indeed an economic system based on mass standardized production demands that this should be so. But inequality remains extreme. The poor are as a whole not getting absolutely poorer, although some may be. But there has been a tendency for their *relative* poverty to increase.

So far we have been concentrating on the unequal distribution of income. But inequality takes on a new dimension when we look at the way in which *wealth* is distributed. Extreme disparities in income are dwarfed by those in the ownership of personal wealth, which are, as a distinguished Cambridge economist has put it, 'really fantastic'.[5] And Professor Meade is not one who is prone to hyperbole or the expression of revolutionary sentiments.

4. Royal Commission, op. cit., and *Social Trends*.
5. J. E. Meade, *Efficiency, Equality and the Ownership of Capital*, Allen & Unwin, 1964.

By personal wealth is meant holdings of physical assets like houses, land and consumer durable goods, and financial assets such as bank and building society deposits, stocks and shares. Dividing the total personal wealth in Britain in 1980 among the adult population as a whole would give an average holding per person of £13,705. The extent to which wealth is unequally held can be seen from government estimates that in 1980 the most wealthy 1 per cent of the population owned 23 per cent of total personal wealth, the most wealthy 10 per cent held over half the total, whilst the bottom 50 per cent held the grand total of 6 per cent of total personal wealth.

The same statistics show that wealth is far more unevenly distributed than income. In 1980, the top 1 per cent of wealth owners owned 23 times as much as the average person. On the other hand the top 1 per cent of income earners earned only 5·2 times as much as the average person. Actual inequalities are probably larger than this because the highest income earners and the wealthiest in Britain have a great incentive to avoid and evade taxes, upon which most of the figures are calculated.

The concentration of wealth in very few hands has certainly been reduced over the years: it has been estimated that in the first decade of the century the top 1 per cent owned 65–70 per cent of total personal wealth. But the evidence also suggests that the trend to increased equality has subsequently been halted, in spite of apparently penal rates of death duties imposed on large estates. What has happened, as with incomes, is that methods of avoidance have become increasingly sophisticated, with the result that further redistribution has largely taken place *within* the top strata of wealth holders through gifts and trust schemes in avoidance of Capital Transfer Tax.

How have these massive inequalities come about? Suppose that we begin with a primitive market economy made up of individuals none of whom possess any wealth and all of whom have equal incomes. How will it develop?[6] At *Stage I*, income differentials will soon emerge – if only because of the uneven dispersion of talents. Similarly, inequality in wealth will also

6. What follows is a stylization of the analysis in Meade, op. cit.

appear, partly because the richer can afford to save more, but also simply as a result of the age distribution of the population – with the old having had more time to accumulate capital than the young. *Stage II* is an interesting one, where a combination of social and genetic factors come into play. Birds of a feather mix together. There will be a tendency for marriages to take place between those of similar 'intelligence' or talents, and between those whose income levels bring them into closest contact. Genetically, the implication seems to be that although, on average, the children of highly intelligent parents will be of lower intelligence than themselves, there is also a greater chance of their offspring being exceptionally intelligent. Thus there are both levelling-up and levelling-down elements at work – but also a polarization of the extremes. To the extent that intelligence and talents are associated with earning power, the overall effect will be disequalizing. *Stage III* introduces the association of earning power with property ownership. Those with higher incomes will not only be able to save more but are likely to save in more profitable ways. *Stage IV* depends on the inheritance system: primogeniture enables a further consolidation of wealth, disequalizing to the extent that the subsequent generations are capable of at least retaining their inherited fortunes. By *Stage V*, the full cumulative forces begin to work. Initial natural advantages leading to accumulated wealth, passed on in the form of inherited riches, generate further acquired advantages of wealth. The rich can buy superior education for their children and set them up in businesses and professions in which the personal contacts between groups of like-minded people are vital. And the 'poor' are further impoverished because the quality of non-private education, for example, is kept low because those very parents most likely to agitate for its improvements, the rich and vocal, are those who have opted out. Finally, by *Stage VI*, there develops an association between earning power, wealth and *ruling* power. The rich become strong enough to inculcate their own élitist ethos into a society and to achieve effective control over the legislature, the administration and mass media in a way best serving their own ends.

All of this happens without any conscious conspiracy on the part of the rich. The argument is simply that, once an initial inequality is established, market forces work to widen rather than diminish the gap between the rich and the poor, the privileged and the underprivileged.

Thus inequalities of income and wealth are mutually reinforcing. In the last chapter we dealt only with disparities in income earned from *work*. But however great the differential between the average worker and the average managing director, it is nothing compared with the income gap between 'earned' and 'unearned' income resulting from ownership or wealth.

But would policies aimed at redistributing wealth be anything more than an emotional gesture? While it is admitted that wealth is concentrated in the hands of a very few, it is often said that to spread it out over the population as a whole would be a mere drop in the ocean. This is simply not true. If wealth in Britain *were* to be equally distributed amongst the adult population, the bottom 50 per cent of wealth owners would see their wealth jump from an average of £411 in 1980 to £13,705 – an increase of £13,294. Assuming the money were invested at a rate of interest of 10 per cent, the average income of the bottom 50 per cent would rise by no less than £25·57 a week.

All this raises the question of economic justice. There is undoubtedly much dissatisfaction, more particularly among the less well-off in our society, with an economic system which generates blatant inequalities. People are concerned less about what is happening to the economy as a whole than about how it affects *them*, where they stand in relation to others, whether or not they are being done down and what they can do about it. This questioning of income and wealth distribution is the natural product of a number of forces which have developed over the years to give people a greater awareness of the total situation and their position in it. 'Universal education has taken away from the minority the power of exclusive knowledge.'[7] In this process the mass media have played an important part.

7. R. Maudling, *The Times*, 12 September 1972.

The downstairs are no longer ignorant of the goings-on up-
stairs. We are all intimately acquainted with the life-styles
of those in different social circumstances from our own. Moreover there has been a marked increase in the power of organized
labour, and modern industry is so complex and interdependent
that it is not merely mass unions who are able to strike a hard
bargain; quite small groups of workers can be equally powerful
if they are engaged in strategically important occupations on
which much larger industries depend.

These momentous changes inevitably subject society to enormous social and economic stresses which can be summed up
in the frank admission of a 'young Conservative lawyer' that
'It's all right when only 5 per cent of the population are grab-
bing, the trouble is when the other 95 per cent start playing
the game.'[8] In this game, inflation plays a stabilizing role in
providing a safety-valve through which a variety of social and
economic tensions can be released. It creates an arena in which
battles can be fought without real bullets. It is a game in which
nearly everyone, or everyone with bargaining strength or vocal
enough to be electorally significant, can at some stage or other
claim to be on the winning side. Admittedly, the gains may
be only ephemeral or even illusory. To a large extent Keynes
was right when he argued that

a demand on the part of the Trade Unions for an increase in money
rates of wages to compensate for every increase in the cost of living
is futile, and greatly to the disadvantage of the working class. Like
the dog in the fable, they lose the substance in gaping at the shadow.
It is true that the better organized sections might benefit at the expense
of other consumers. But except as an effort at group selfishness, as
a means of hustling someone else out of the queue, it is a mug's game
to play. In their minds and hearts the leaders of the Trade Unions
know this as well as anyone else. They do not want what they ask.
But they dare not abate their demands until they know what alternative
policy is offered.[9]

That alternative can only be one which openly examines the

8. Quoted in G. Turner, *Towards a New Philosophy for Industrial Society.*
9. J. M. Keynes, *How to Pay for the War*, Macmillan, 1940.

way in which incomes are now determined and questions the
distribution of income and wealth which results from it. Widespread dissatisfaction with the present outcome is shown by
the results of a 1973 study[10] which suggested that only 19
per cent of the population thought that the current share-out
of wages among different jobs in Britain was at all fair. And
this study dealt only with the distribution of wage income.
It can hardly be doubted that, if the same question had been
asked about the share-out between wage and management
incomes and between incomes from work and wealth, and about
the distribution of wealth itself, an even greater proportion
would have been of the opinion that the situation was iniquitous.

We have already looked at the facts of the matter and argued
that the economic case put forward by supporters of inequality
– that, for example, it provides incentives and a source of capital
accumulation without which the economy would function very
ineffectively – is far from convincing. Nor is there any clear
moral justification for major disparities. And yet the burden
of proof surely lies with these opponents of equality. As Sir
Isaiah Berlin has put it: 'If I have a cake and there are ten
persons among whom I wish to divide it, then if I give exactly
one tenth to each, this will not, at any rate automatically, call
for justification; whereas if I depart from this principle of equal
division I am expected to produce a special reason.'[11]

Presumption and morality both point towards egalitarianism.
And so, for that matter, does traditional economic theory –
although, in providing an analytical framework in which inequalities can be understood, it has frequently been taken as
implicitly justifying them. In fact, however, classical economic
thinking is logically egalitarian in its implications. Thus in the
theory of consumer behaviour there is a concept of 'diminishing
marginal utility', which simply means that the more you have
of something the less you desire a bit more of it. It is a concept

10. *Report on the Study of Some Aspects of National Job Evaluation*, North
Paul and Associates Ltd, 1973.

11. Quoted in A. B. Atkinson, *Unequal Shares*, Allen Lane The Penguin Press,
1972, p. 79.

which can be applied not only to bread or television sets or ballpoint pens, but also to money itself (except in the case of misers). The result is that to give a pound to a very rich man will afford him far less satisfaction than giving it to a very poor man. Similarly, taking away a pound from the rich and redistributing it to the poor will be likely to increase total satisfaction (provided that they have the same capacity for enjoyment). It was on this basis that Sir Dennis Robertson, one of the more 'reactionary' and brilliant economists of the orthodox school, used to have to argue for equality in terms of 'passionate reluctance'.

How then could inequalities be reduced? Three broad means can be distinguished. The first is one which can only be effective in the very long run, and that is to attack the causes of social immobility which are a major source of disparities. This can only be achieved by fundamental reform of the educational system, substantially to widen access to a range of occupations now confined to a privileged few. In practical terms this must mean the abolition of a private fee-paying system of education run in parallel with that provided by the State. Whether by educating their children privately parents actually buy them a higher quality of education or merely a passport into restricted social circles, there can be no doubt that the continued existence of public schools is a central element in the process of self-perpetuating inequalities. In fact, egalitarianism requires much more than equality of educational opportunity. What is needed is positive discrimination in favour of initially less-privileged groups – quite the opposite of the situation as it is, where children born in industrial slums or coloured ghettoes are likely to find themselves still further under-privileged by attending overcrowded and antiquated schools unable to attract good teaching staff easily.

A second approach is to treat the symptoms. If the gap between incomes from work is thought to be intolerably wide, it is open to the State to siphon off excessive earnings through more progressive taxation. There are certainly difficulties, because, as a general rule, the higher the income, the greater the possibilities for tax evasion and tax avoidance. And, once again, at times we have moved in the opposite direction. Thus, for example, the tax changes operative in 1979–80 announced in the 1979 budget amounted to a substantial redistribution to high-income groups.

At a time when the government was urging pay restraint, particularly for ordinary working people, income tax changes then beginning to take effect were increasing the after-tax earnings of a married couple with no children by 6 per cent if they earned £2,000 a year, 5 per cent if they earned £5,000 or £10,000 a year, but by 19 per cent if they earned £15,000 a year, 24 per cent if they earned £25,000 a year and a staggering 55 per cent for the lucky £50,000-a-year earners.

The third approach is a more direct one. *If* we are aiming at greater equality, then it is more logical to reduce pre-tax disparities rather than try to soak them away through taxation. But how can this be done in a situation in which, as we have already pointed out, top-income groups largely determine their own rates of pay? This can only come about if the government itself accepts full responsibility for determining differentials *or* if a public consensus emerges which puts social pressure on high-income groups to accept lower remuneration *or* if the power structure is changed so that workers in an industry are involved in the process of determining not only their own wage rates but those above and below them.

The examples of Sweden and Israel suggest that there would be powerful resistance from professional groups threatened by policies aimed at achieving substantially greater equality. In Britain, on the other hand, even the principles involved are not in the forefront of public debate, let alone the practical difficulties in reducing inequality. In the past, we were content to pay lip-service to greater equality as a vague ideal and pretend that our taxation system was gradually bringing it about. More recently, the ideal itself has been rejected in the official emphasis on the importance of creating greater 'incentives'.

It is not therefore that we do not *know* how to reduce inequalities in income and wealth. A great deal of work has already been done devising ways in which greater equality could be achieved. What is lacking is the political will to take effective action. The better-off in society, for very understandable reasons, are reluctant to see greater economic equality, whilst the less well-off in society passively accept the current economic order. Indeed, the lower-paid themselves often evince dismay when they learn that high-income earners pay high marginal income tax rates – up to 60 per cent at present in Britain. What they see is that, if they were earning that much, they would be most annoyed that the State would be taking 60p in every £1 of any increase in income. What they fail to see is that their relative poverty is ultimately caused by the relative affluence of others. If there is a relatively fixed national cake to share out, the few can only get large shares if the rest are left with below-average-sized shares.

Present policies on taxation, government spending and the share of output of the public sector are likely to increase inequalities in society. We have already mentioned the enormous income tax gains made by higher-income earners in the 1979 budget. But inequalities are increasing in more hidden ways too. Take, for example, the provision of education and health services. No one could deny that in these two areas enormous advances have been made since the war. But can we be satisfied that sufficiently rapid progress has been made in maintaining the quality of these services at a level which is appropriate to our growing material affluence? The National Health Service is constantly under fire – for its lack of comprehensiveness, its delays, its intrusions on personal privacy and dignity, for being over-pressured and consequently lacking in compassion. Vast areas of educational underprivilege continue to exist in the 1980s. The variations in the quality of schooling both within towns and between different parts of the country are often extreme. *One* of the reasons why these deficiencies have not been made good is the fact that education and medical care are also provided on a private, fee-paying basis by the market. Despite the extension of state education and health services, parallel systems of public schools and private provision for health have not only continued to exist but indeed seem to grow from strength to strength. Given a starting point of highly unequally distributed income and wealth, the result is predictable. The few who can afford to cater for their education and health needs by forking out of their own pockets tend to opt out of the state system. But it is these middle- and upper-income groups who generally have the strongest views about standards, who are most vociferous and capable of bringing pressure to bear on the relevant authorities to ensure that services of an acceptable quality are provided. Not only, then, is the provision of private education and medical care a direct expression of existing inequality. Not only does it perpetuate that inequality by giving the offspring of the privileged minority a better start in life. There is, on top of that, a detrimental feed-back for the state services – in the lack of push for improvement in their quality which would certainly come about if everyone, regardless of their social and economic position, had to use them.

It is difficult not to conclude that, as a rough rule of thumb, the greater the proportion of output which goes to private rather than collective consumption, the stronger will be the forces making for the perpetuation of inequality.

And if we are moving towards a more free-market economy, those inequalities become increasingly significant in limiting access to the consumption of goods and services to those with the ability to pay.

Is this the sort of society that we wish to create – in which a significant minority of the population are relatively disenfranchised, even in key areas of basic needs such as health, education and housing? Is it acceptable that the poor should be denied the best available medical care or educational provision? Can we tolerate a situation where the majority live in decent private housing while the rest scramble for a declining stock of under-maintained council housing? One nation or two – that is the question.

14

Who Wants Full Employment?

For most of the post-war period, maintaining a high level of employment has been given the highest priority among the objectives of economic policy. That was as it should be. Unemployment, quite apart from being absurdly wasteful, has been the most humanly degrading feature of twentieth-century capitalism. It is an evil which the increased economic understanding of the Keynesian revolution seemed to make it possible for governments largely to eradicate. And the employment performance of the economy in the first couple of decades after the war was certainly dramatically better than it had ever been before.

Subsequently, there were increased doubts expressed about just how compatible full employment was with the control of inflation, getting the balance of payments right and the achievement of rapid economic growth. Governments came to espouse the idea that there might be awkward 'trade-offs' between their policy objectives – that, for example, curbing price increases might involve having a somewhat larger pool of unemployment. They therefore did not always try to maximize employment, but the higher level of 'politically acceptable' unemployment of the late 1960s and early 1970s remained very low in comparison with what was customary in the pre-war period.

More recently, unemployment has risen to levels which in that earlier period would have been regarded as a sure recipe for nothing less than revolution. There would have been general agreement at the time that 3 or 4 million out of work would never again be tolerated by the British people. And yet the unthinkable has become a reality. The 'intolerable' has, in effect,

been endorsed by the electorate and there appears to be a growing resignation to the proposition that full employment is a
matter of the past, a brief triumph over a less comfortable
natural order which is now re-establishing itself.

Can it be true? Is there really no future prospect that full
employment will one day be re-achieved, with young people
leaving school or college quickly finding work to suit their
qualifications, and older workers able and willing to leave one
form of employment for another in the reasonably secure knowledge that alternatives will be available?

No one *knows* the answer to that question. But it is important
to see the scenarios that seem to be implied in the thinking
of the various broad schools of economic opinion.

Employment and Monetarism

Monetarism, as we have already seen, is essentially a *technical*
theory about the nature of inflation – that its causes lie in
excessive increases in the money supply. But in practice, of
course, it has been associated with a much wider political
ideology.

Thus it has become equated with the view that price stability
is the paramount priority of government economic policy. To
the extent that other macro-objectives are discussed within the
monetarist framework, it is claimed that *only* with 'sound
money' can the competitiveness be restored that will ultimately
lead to sustained economic growth. So far as employment is
concerned, there are occasional references to the transitoriness
of present levels of unemployment and the assertion that it
is *only* by pursuit of present policies that 'real jobs' will be
created.

But full employment no longer features in government policy
statements even as a *goal* ultimately to be achieved. Ministerial
pronouncements scrupulously avoid prediction about future
changes in the unemployment level or the setting of time-
targets for its reduction, let alone its elimination. Gone, in
fact, is any commitment to a full-employment objective and the

acceptance by government of responsibility for its achievement.

This is not surprising and indeed is intellectually consistent with the monetarist doctrine. Monetarists argue that the economy is a fundamentally stable system provided that market forces are allowed the fullest possible sway. Thus government spending should be reduced to what can be financed by lower levels of taxation. Resources should be diverted from the inefficient public sector to the 'wealth-creating' private sector. Individual markets should be freed from bureaucratic controls.

And unemployment will settle at its 'natural' rate. The market for labour will clear itself provided only that those seeking work are prepared to accept that wage rate which equates the supply of those wanting jobs with the demand for them. Currently, wage rates are above that level. Monetarists hope that the experience of recent years will bring a new sense of 'realism' to wage bargaining so that worker expectations of the appropriate going rate are reduced. Governments can assist by legal reform limiting the bargaining power of unions. But beyond that, so monetarists argue, the level of employment is not a matter for which governments can accept responsibility.

The whole monetarist-cum-market edifice rests on highly questionable or debatable propositions. With respect to values, is it *still* the general view after the experience of the past decade that high unemployment is preferable to high inflation? (Anyway, we still do not know the precise relationship between jobs and prices; all that has been painfully re-learned is that crude deflation of the economy does ultimately slow down the inflationary process.) *Technically* the view that it is the money supply that causes inflation remains, to say the least, unproven. And *institutionally*, we must surely be even more sceptical than before about the government's ability to regulate the money supply or create a situation in which wage rates are reducible. Recent evidence suggests that even when the *rate* of unemployment increase slows down, earnings begin to rise again. Those who have been lucky enough to hold on to their jobs no longer find that the ugly threat of unemployment is sufficient reason for them to alter their previous attitudes and behaviour.

We have been engaged in an experiment, indeed we have been its subjects, the huge human and social costs of which have become increasingly clear – although the final outcome, strictly speaking, remains uncertain. But what is worrying, from our present point of view, is that the restoration of full employment, far from being a prime objective, is not even explicitly on the current political agenda.

Employment and Keynesianism

For Keynes himself, wrestling with the illogicality of an economic system gone so radically wrong as to throw millions out of work, employment creation was a necessary condition for saving the capitalist system. Given his view that the greater part of unemployment was due solely to demand-deficiency, *any* increased activity would be sufficient to generate a multiplied effect on employment levels. Pay men to dig holes in the ground and fill them up again, and their increased spending would stimulate increased output and employment in more productive occupations. As Keynes pointed out, earlier economic systems had stumbled upon their own solutions to the problem: 'Ancient Egypt was doubly fortunate, and doubtless owed to this its fabled wealth, in that it possessed *two* activities, namely, pyramid building as well as the search for precious metals, the fruits of which, since they could not serve the needs of man by being consumed, did not stale with abundance. The Middle Ages built cathedrals and sang dirges.' But, as Keynes went on to point out: 'It is not reasonable, however, that a sensible community should be content to remain dependent on such fortuitous and often wasteful mitigations when once we understand the influences upon which effective demand depends.'[1]

For Keynesians, the economy remains a fundamentally un-

1. J. M. Keynes, *General Theory of Employment, Interest and Money*, p. 131.

stable system and governments need to intervene forcefully to compensate for the failures of the free-market mechanism. Keynesians today continue to argue that an expansion and regulation of demand is an essential prerequisite for returning to full employment. But most recognize that this would be a necessary rather than a sufficient condition for sustained economy recovery, and that it would need to be accompanied by a variety of supportive policies. As we have seen, three obvious problems would be likely to arise.

(i) Given the high U.K. propensity to import, coupled with the present weakness of home manufacturing industry, expansion would quickly result in a serious current account deficit on the balance of payments. The extent of this problem would be greatly reduced if only the leading industrial nations simultaneously pursued reflationary strategies but there seems little prospect for the moment of such concerted action in the form of global or even European Keynesianism.

A British government going it alone along the Keynesian road would therefore be severely constrained in this respect and would need to contemplate devaluation or import controls (together with limitation on further foreign investment) in order to offset the weakness in the balance of payments which already exists but is currently masked by high unemployment.

(ii) While there is no reason to assume that Keynesian expansion would be inherently inflationary in its early stages, when there would be substantial excess capacity in industry and ample supplies of labour, bottlenecks and the impact of higher import prices as a result of devaluation would ultimately lead to those cost-inflationary pressures that earlier Keynesian governments failed to cope with fully. There seems to be little hope of escape from the introduction of a prices and incomes policy as a necessary corollary to an expansionist approach. Such policies have failed in the past. But politically, when the consequences of the alternative should have been fully recognized, the timing might now be more propitious than ever before.

(iii) Expansionary fiscal policy might no longer work because of an inadequate *response* on the part of home producers to a demand stimulus. To some extent, the experience of monetarism is to blame – in weakening the industrial base from which such expansion would have to be launched and in instilling entrepreneurial doubts that a Keynesian recovery can be sustained without uncontrollable inflation. Such doubts could well lead to an abortive 'wait and see' attitude and to a reluctance to invest in higher capacity that might subsequently prove excessive.

If that were to prove the case, then the answer could lie only in more systematic extension of the role of the State in the investment process. Indeed, in the not dissimilar circumstances of the 1930s, Keynes himself contemplated that possibility which to him must have been an unpalatable one. His position was unequivocal but has since been little noted, let alone allowed to serve as the basis for policy. 'I conceive, therefore,' he wrote in the *General Theory*, 'that a somewhat comprehensive socialisation of investment will prove the only means of securing an approximation to full employment.'[2] Far from relying exclusively on general demand-management manipulation, Keynes clearly foresaw the need for supply-side measures to overcome institutional constraints on higher investment – measures far more radical than any post-war Labour government subsequently attempted.

Employment: A Third View

A third possibility arises because, so it is claimed, we are now in the initial throes of a fundamental technological revolution – which will make impossible the continued job-creation of the kind to which we have been accustomed in the past

The automation of the future must be distinguished from simple mechanization not only in the sheer extent to which machines will be capable of taking over from labour in the ordinary production processes, but also in the width of its

2. p. 378.

potential application (over a great range of hitherto labour-intensive service occupations) and the computerization of 'higher' areas of skill and decision-taking, as well as the more mundane operations.

However, automation 'scares' of this kind have been aired for decades and many economists are still inclined to take an optimistic view of the probable outcome. They regurgitate the arguments which they put forward against the nineteenth-century Luddites. Then, it was claimed, mechanization was bound to cause unemployment. No, said the economists. What will happen is that mechanization will lead to higher productivity and falling prices. At lower prices, more goods will be bought – and both more machines *and* more workers will be required. In the end, the economists were right, although there was a great deal of temporary technological unemployment and social distress during the transitional period to industrialization.

But is the argument equally applicable to the sort of technological revolution through which we are now passing? The pessimistic view is that new technology coupled with the continued underlying growth in the world workforce may render both the Keynesian and market-clearing mechanisms equally irrelevant in solving future unemployment problems. Thus, it is argued, the labour saving involved in automated production is of a quite different *order* from what has gone before. This is true both quantitatively (the reduction in workforce needed can be quite dramatic) and qualitatively – because automation does not make just unskilled and semi-skilled workers redundant but extends into the echelons of lower management itself.

The economists' principle might still hold good. Reduced prices might stimulate demand to a level at which it would still be possible for everyone to be employed in automated plants. But the level of production which that would entail would have to be of quite astronomical proportions, requiring enormous quantities of capital to generate full employment along Keynesian lines at the new high level of technology. Perhaps demand *could* be created to absorb that output. But would it make sense to do so? Is there *no* limit to our material acquisitiveness or to the natural resources which would be needed?

Then again, much current unemployment, as we have seen, is concentrated in the unskilled, young and aged groups of workers who, in a modern technological economy, have depressingly little to offer. Automation will make redundant more of these workers, those with what are now regarded as considerable mechanical skills, and also clerical and lower management staff. If they are to be re-employed, they will have to learn new and appropriate skills. But, as Mishan puts it, 'it is far from being impossible that in the not too-distant future a large proportion of the adult population would be *unemployable* simply because they would not be endowed with the innate capacities necessary to acquire the highly developed mental skills which may be called for by a more complex technology.'[3]

The basic question, as Professor Meade points out,[4] is whether 'Chips and Robots' will 'make Men less valuable in production than Machinery – whether, that is to say, it will raise the return on capital relatively to the real wage offered to the worker – and if so by how much.'

In other words, the increased profitability of capital (held in relatively few hands) would lead to one of two possible dangers. 'Either competition among workers for the small number of jobs would reduce the real wage absolutely to a very low level or else, if by trade union or similar action the real wage was held up, there would be a large volume of involuntary unemployment among those who were not privileged to get the few jobs available at the fixed rate of pay.'

With production concentrated in a relatively small number of very technologically sophisticated plants, the great majority would be faced with alternative nightmares – mass unemployment, or what Professor Meade in an earlier work dubbed the 'Brave New Capitalist's Paradise'.

3. E. J. Mishan, *The Costs of Economic Growth*, Penguin Books, 1969, p. 228.

4. James Meade, 'A New Keynesian Approach to Full Employment', *Lloyds Bank Review*, October 1983, p. 11.

Wage rates would thus be depressed; there would have to be a large expansion of the production of the labour-intensive goods and services which were in high demand by the few multi-multi-millionaires; we would be back in a super-world of an immiserized proletariat and of butlers, footmen, kitchen maids, and other hangers-on.[5]

The Distribution of Work

Suppose that full employment in the conventional sense proves to be unattainable. Then it is vital that whatever volume of work *is* available should be distributed equitably among those who want it. That might entail redefining what we mean by full employment. In Britain today, it means finding jobs for some 26 million people – working forty hours a week for forty-eight weeks a year over a fifty-year working life. But that is very different from its meaning had the term ever been applied in the nineteenth century – with the very different numbers involved, child labour, long working hours and lower expectation of life. Thus the notion of full employment is based on social conventions or norms which are themselves capable of being reformulated. Is it not time to think much more seriously in terms of a shorter working day, a shorter working week, a shorter working life? Possible technological unemployment can thereby be avoided if some of the benefits of higher productivity are taken, not in increased output, but in greater leisure.

However, it is important that such leisure should be voluntary rather than the involuntary inactivity of a growing proportion of the workforce imposed by mass unemployment. New mechanisms will have to be devised for ensuring that work- or leisure-sharing are fairly distributed, because the prospects for this being achieved within the present market framework seem extraordinarily unfavourable. Such a framework embodies basic conflicts of interests – between different groups of workers, and between capital and labour.

(i) *Worker* v. *Worker* Although lip-service may be paid to

5. *Efficiency, Equality of the Ownership of Property*, Allen & Unwin, p. 33.

the concept of work-sharing, it is not in fact a very likely outcome in a market economy with powerful and sectional trade unions. It is much more probable that trade unions in modern technological industries (representing as they do the interests of their current members rather than potential members or the working class as a whole) will work to limit the spread of employment, by achieving high wages for their own workers. They are, after all, in a strong bargaining position to do so. Labour productivity (output per man) in such industries is likely to be very high – partly because of the skills of the workers employed but also because they are fortunate enough to be working with large quantities of capital. High wages can be justified on grounds of productivity and employers are not averse to paying them, since wages form only a small proportion of their total costs. Indeed it is vital for managements to maintain industrial peace because of the enormous costs of allowing expensive plant to lie idle for any length of time.

(ii) *Capital* v. *Labour*   If Professor Meade is correct in his fear that new technology will result in a marked shift of income to those owning capital from those only contributing their own labour to the productive process, then we shall see an even more disparate distribution of income and wealth than that which we analysed in Chapters 12 and 13.

Such an outcome would not only be morally intolerable. Its divisiveness would be such that it is difficult to imagine how the ensuing pressures and resentment could conceivably be contained within our present social fabric. And yet that is the course on which we may now be set.

If such a disaster is to be averted, it may be necessary to contemplate policies of regulating income determination and widespread social ownership of capital – not as political dogmas but as the only means of ensuring a workable and relatively stable social system.

Moves in such a direction may be repugnant to many and certainly cut across the grain of the prevailing political ethos. But in the same way that Keynes argued in the 1930s that capitalism could only be saved by an abandonment of *laissez-*

faire, so today even more radical means may be implied if our objective is to sustain a society in which most of us can happily exist and of which we can be reasonably proud.

The Quality of Work

Concentrating on the overall employment total conceals the question of what employment is *for* – what it is that people are producing when they work. This is a matter which we shall be looking at in the following chapter. It is also important to ask questions about the *content* of work. What is happening to its intensity and tempo? How far does the work which people do afford them interest and satisfaction? Do their jobs leave them with the capacity fully to enjoy their leisure? How easy is it for people to find, not just any jobs, but jobs which they think match their abilities and temperaments?

We have been stressing the importance of keeping the re-achievement of 'full employment', however defined, prominently on the agenda of future political action. But, with that said, it is still sensible to ask how far full employment should itself be regarded as an *end* of economic policy. After all, for most people their jobs are simply the unavoidable drudgery by which they achieve an acceptable standard of living and an important element in their social relationships. Only for a lucky few is their work a source of personal satisfaction or fulfilment. In either case, employment is surely primarily a *means* rather than an end; we work in order to achieve a variety of ends. Even when full employment was the norm, it made sense to argue that far more attention should be paid to the *nature* of employment. That should still be a prime concern today.

As a starting-point, in this age of exploding technologies, it is worth reviewing the impact of technical progress on the working lives of ordinary people.

Taking a broad view, the benefits from technical change have clearly been enormous. First of all, it has been possible through mechanization to replace a whole host of dirty, unpleasant, physically demanding jobs which were once done by men and women. Moreover, the increase in material wellbeing over the past centuries must be attributed, above all, to increased division of labour. Specialization by workers in particular tasks has been the major cause of the enormous increases in productivity which have taken place. Apart from the obvious improvements in efficiency which come from specialization, through greater dexterity and learning through experience, greater division of labour means job *simplification*. And once that happens, once a complex production process is broken down into its component parts, it is possible to introduce mechanization.

But what has been lost in the process? It is easy nostalgically to extol the virtues of an idyllic pre-industrial age.

Two centuries ago, before the 'industrial revolution' was properly launched, a skilled workman in this country was a craftsman. Whether he worked in wood, clay, leather, stone, metal or glass, he was the master of his material, and the thing he produced grew in his hands from the substance of the earth to the finished article. He was ever-mindful that he was a member of an honoured craft; that he had reached his position after a long apprenticeship; and he took legitimate pride in the excellence of his work ... Whatever else may have been lacking in that smaller scale of society in which the yeoman tilled the soil and masters and apprentices worked with patient skill at this craft, there was always this unassailable self-respect and, therefore, that abiding sense of security which is no common thing in the feverish jostling world of today.[6]

Well, perhaps it wasn't *quite* like that. But there is nonetheless enough substance in the point for us to ask whether the division of labour in modern industrial societies has now proceeded to a degree which is almost self-defeating. Where work has been reduced to the endless repetition of a simple mindless task, where workers are little more than machine-minders, is it any longer possible to take pride in one's work or to derive any creative satisfaction from it?

The matter can be viewed first of all from the aspect of

6. Mishan, op. cit., pp. 206–9.

sheer economic efficiency. Workers utterly remote from the final product, engaged in what they consider an inevitable but meaningless drudge, are not likely to approach their work particularly conscientiously or responsibly. Mistakes are made, but nobody very much cares. (It is said about cars, for example, that the real 'duds' are those which come off the Monday assembly line.) The upshot is that either more resources have to be devoted to elaborate inspection procedures to maintain quality control, or the quality of the final product is unreliable. Moreover, the pent-up frustrations of endlessly monotonous working patterns must in the end boil over. Disputes, stoppages and industrial tension are at least partly attributable to the need to break the monotony of an otherwise never-ending routine.

These are facts which are now beginning to be recognized by industrial managements. In the nineteenth century it took a long time before employers realized that higher wages, far from pricing them into bankruptcy, were in fact a source of higher profits from greater productivity. Workers who earned enough to feed and look after themselves adequately turned out, incredibly, to be better at doing their jobs. Similarly today, there are enterprises where it is appreciated that greater job satisfaction may be an important element in further productivity increase.

The Volvo company in Sweden, for example, has built a car plant at Kalmar which challenges all the traditional principles which have dominated motor-car economics since Henry Ford. What they have done is no less than to abandon the conventional assembly line, manned by workers each performing repetitively a simple task as the car passes by and having little or no contact with those working alongside them. Instead, Volvo see the workforce as split into groups of between fifteen and twenty-five. The assembly line is replaced by a system of components shunted round on electric trollies which are moved into the groups' working bays when required. The work which the group performs is a major production stage – the installation, for instance, of a complete electrical system.

How they do it, how they divide the work amongst themselves, is up to them.

This is anti-specialization. In terms of capital outlay, the Kalmar factory cost nearly 10 per cent more than the traditional lay-out. But Volvo are clearly hoping that the new experiment will contribute towards reducing some of the problems which have plagued them and other motor-car manufacturers in the past – widespread absenteeism and high labour turnover (the particularly traumatic year for Volvo was 1969, with an incredible 52 per cent turnover in its workforce). On top of that, Volvo had increasing difficulty in attracting people to work in the factories at all. With higher education and living standards than our own, Swedish workers spurned the monotony of the assembly line, and the Swedish industry was increasingly manned by Finns and Yugoslavs.

A decade later, Volvo's plant has proved itself highly successful. Absenteeism has declined. Increases in productivity have fully justified Volvo's initial investment. In 1981–2, productivity was 20 per cent higher than at the conventionally designed Volvo plant at Torslanda, both plants carrying the same mix of car models. Such experiments – and there are a sprinkling of others – are wholly to be welcomed. But that does not mean that we should neglect situations in which job enrichment may *not* pay. Surely as a society we are now rich enough for methods of humanizing work to be thought worthwhile in themselves.

What we have to do is to get away from thinking that big is necessarily good, that massive scale and extreme specialization are technological imperatives. There *is* an alternative technology which would evolve once workers (and managers) were regarded as individuals rather than faceless 'labour inputs'. But efforts in this direction in devising more humanized techniques are bound to be limited until the nature of work is emphasized as the proper objective of employment policy.

Take, for example, the question of the hours which people work. Present techniques generally demand great regularity – so many hours a day (or, in some cases, a night), so many days a week and so many weeks a year. But why? Why shouldn't individuals be allowed to work the *number* of hours they like, and *when* they like. Here again, a start has been made. The 1970s saw a mushrooming of flexi-time arrangements, particularly for office workers. These allowed workers to start and finish work when they wished, so long as they completed the requisite number of hours in a week. But why should this very popular arrangement not be extended to manufacturing production? Certainly it would be difficult in a situation where workers combine with highly expensive capital equipment. But once the principle was accepted, technology would have to be adapted accordingly. And this is as it should be – that technology adjusts to people rather than the other way round.

The nature of the work people do is closely related to the importance which they attach to leisure and the ways in which they use it. It was Marx who said that 'the production of too many useful things results in too many useless people'. The ethos of the modern industrial economy creates the danger that in their striving to acquire more and more goods people will become increasingly incapable of enjoying them. With their sensibility blunted by the dullness of their working environment, it is not surprising that many have such difficulty in adjusting to retirement or using their time off in a satisfying way. Once again, as Galbraith points out, greater flexibility of working hours has an important contribution to make towards creating a more positive attitude to leisure opportunities:

The employed person should be accorded a much wider set of options than at present between work and goods on the one hand and leisure on the other. But the options should not be confined to the work week. This is a poor unit around which to organize the effective use of leisure time; it has long been a perquisite of high social, educational or financial position that life – holidays, travel, tasks – is planned in terms of months or years. All individuals, in return for a lower annual pay, should have the option of several months' paid vacation. And all should similarly have the option of extended leaves of absence. The employees exercising these options would not be favoured in compensation per hour worked. What they are offered is the opportunity

of choosing absence and exemption from toil in various forms as an
alternative to earnings. There would be some inconvenience. But to
fail to allow such choice – to be guided by the belief that everyone
should work a standard week and year – is to make the needs of the
industrial system, not the opportunity of the individual to fashion his
own existence, the ruling social concern. Men who speak much of
liberty should allow and even encourage it.[7]

In particular what this vista opens up is the possibility of
a new approach to education. At present education is largely
confined to the years preceding working life. But there is no
reason why it should not be an ongoing process to which people
can return as and when they please. Here, too, it is Sweden
which has pioneered the notion that equality of opportunity
means equal chances for young and old alike. Swedish 'second-
path' philosophy ensures that there is a wide range of educational openings for adults, either for return to secondary schools
or for mature entry into the universities or for industrial retraining.

There are some signs of a growing awareness that work is
not an end in itself. Among the ranks of the unemployed are
some older workers who have welcomed redundancy as the
opportunity to pursue their other interests, and *some* young
people who positively reject the possibility, even if it were open
to them, of mindless work of the traditional kind. But for the
great majority of the jobless their enforced inactivity is a cruel
parody of 'leisure' because they live in a social context where
leisure involves more rather than less spending.

It is possible that the application of new technology in
coming decades will afford the opportunity of redefining full
employment in ways that reduce the proportion of people's time
spent in paid work and increase their scope and capacity to
enjoy other satisfying forms of 'activity'. But for the fruits
of new technology to be equitably shared there might need to
be a fundamental change in our present system of income

7. J. K. Galbraith, *The New Industrial State*, Penguin Books, 1969, p. 369.

distribution, an increasing divorce of 'income' from the 'work' with which in the past it has always been associated.[8]

And beyond that, as we have already suggested, the potentially divisive effects of technology in future years can be avoided only by greater worker involvement in the productive process – not only a greater say in the objectives of the enterprise and the ways in which it achieves them, but *capital*-sharing to resolve the deep-rooted alienation of labour from capital and the social and economic tensions and conflicts which result from it. As Dr Ota Sik has put it: 'Wage earners are interested only in increasing their wages. They have no direct interest in capital, the growth of capital, the use of profits or decisions on investments.'[9] And this is as true in those communist countries where capital has been taken over by the State as it is in the industrial economies of the West. It holds good as much in our own nationalized industries as it does in the private sector.

'Only where man has an immediate economic interest in the future development of an enterprise, in investment, in the effectivity of new capital equipment and so on, will he gradually begin to be master of his own conditions of production.'[10]

In other words, what is needed is not simply greater participation, the occasional worker-director on the board of a company, but the dispersion of power throughout enterprises as a whole. Such a programme of radical reform would certainly arouse violent opposition from those powerful and deeply entrenched interests which are the major beneficiaries of our present system, and much could be written about the political and practical mechanics of bringing about such fundamental changes. But first it is important to debate the principle itself; here again, as with many of the other 'big' questions we have touched upon, what is disturbing is that in Britain today there is so little open public discussion even about whether it is *right* that democracy should stop at the polling-booth and that the economy should be governed according to a quite different set of values.

8. A. Gorz, *Farewell to the Working Class*, Pluto Press, 1982.

9. O. Sik, *The Times*, 4 October 1972.

10. Ibid.

15

Behind the Growth Index

Recent experience, beginning in the 1970s with the ending of an era of cheap energy and culminating in a deep recession compounded by perverse government policies, has created a mood in which any evidence of *growth* in the economy is hailed as a significant achievement, an indication that we are on the road to recovery.

And yet during those post-war decades when the major industrial economies not only expected regular annual increases in their levels of output but actively strove to accelerate their rates of economic growth, there were those prepared to question such obsessive 'Growthmanship'. Early doubts about the conventional enthusiasm for growth were expressed by J. K. Galbraith in his *Affluent Society*.[1] Later E. J. Mishan's *Cost of Economic Growth* opened up fresh areas of debate. Galbraith was largely concerned with the distortions created by the growth process – seeing 'private affluence and public squalor' as its inevitable byproduct. Mishan was even more caustic: 'There may be doubts amongst philosophers and heart-searching amongst poets, [but] to the multitude the kingdom of God is to be realized here, and now, on this earth; and it is to be realized via technological innovation, and at an exponential rate.'[2] Mishan's revulsion against 'growthmania' was total; for him, the answer to the question 'What conceivable alternative could there be to economic growth?' was obvious – we should contemplate the opposite policy of no-growth. Concerned about the depletion of global resources or sickened by the gross affluence of

1. Hamish Hamilton, 1958; Pelican Books, 1970.
2. Mishan, op. cit., p. 28.

modern industrial societies, the conservationists and anti-materialists were quick to join the bandwagon. But there was also a spirited defence of growth from those who argued that, although growth may create problems, increased output is also still the chief way of solving them. They further pointed out that the anti-growth mantle sat most easily on those who already enjoyed substantial opulence and saw their amenity threatened by its extension to the less fortunate.

But today, implicit in both monetarist and Keynesian proposals for dealing with our present plight is a desire to restore the economy to a steadily rising growth trend. Whether that is attainable remains debatable. But is it anyway what we want? Despite the current mood of pessimism and the weakness of the economy, national income will almost certainly be higher in ten years' time than it is today. But will we be better-off?

This last question might seem a very odd one, but then the growth index is itself a very odd way of measuring anything (other than the increase in the total value of goods and services produced – which is what it is). Unfortunately, observers are seldom content to leave it at that. Such a heroic statistic as the growth in Gross National Product must, they feel, be of far-reaching significance. And so the process of interpretation begins. In no time at all, economic growth becomes synonymous with higher standards of living, economic progress and increases in economic welfare.

To see how misleading the growth index can be, consider the cautionary tale of a country which, at one time, used to pass under the name of Innocentia. Many years ago, life in Innocentia was simple – which is not to say idyllic, because, as economic historians are quick to remind us, the standard of living at that time was evidently far below that of today. The population was grouped into villages and small towns, and production consisted solely of basic goods – food, clothing and shelter. There was enough, and it was sufficiently well distributed, to provide everyone with primitive comfort. So far as we can tell, there was 'full employment' in the sense that all who wanted work could get it. But the Innocentians do not seem to have been a very industrious people: twenty hours was an average working week and a good many weeks were taken off for holidays and festivals. It has been estimated that the value of output (the G.N.P.) was then about £10,000m. a year.

What brought about the dramatic transformation of this primitive and backward society into the modern industrial State it is today was the invention and subsequent exploitation of a revolutionary new product – Candy Floss. Production first took place on the outskirts of a small northern township, and almost overnight Floss took Innocentia by storm. Demand seemed insatiable and all over the country firms sprang up producing a whole range of Floss products – natural, instant, dehydrated, frozen.

Naturally, these new enterprises were generally anxious to site themselves close to the market and this had far-reaching consequences for the Innocentian economy. Site values in the centres of towns and villages were bid up by the competing Floss producers, with the long-term result that workers, faced by a sharp rise in urban house prices, were gradually forced out into suburbia. This in turn involved new forms of expenditure – on roads and public and private transport to facilitate the journey to work and the movement of goods to final consumers.

Moreover, with more and more workers being absorbed by the new Floss enterprises and by the transport and communications sector, output per man in the traditional basic goods industries had to be considerably increased. This was initially achieved by the introduction of a new forty-hour working week.

At this stage, some thirty years after the start of the economic revolution, the Innocentian G.N.P. had risen substantially:

	(£m.)
Basic goods	10,000
Floss sector	10,000
Transport and communications	5,000
	25,000

Subsequent Innocentian development was landmarked by four major crises. First, there was a point at which the Innocentians at long last seemed Floss-weary – it appeared that demand *had* finally been satisfied. But the crisis was short-lived as enterprising Floss producers mounted massive advertising campaigns extolling the virtues of Floss consumption and also put a great deal of money into devising new Floss uses. Demand began to grow again as consumers turned to Floss fabrics, Floss cosmetics, Floss paints and a whole range of other startling and attractive new products.

Second, a dramatic breakthrough in Floss technology led to sharply rising unemployment (rather than a reversion to the previously shorter working week which might have been a more sensible response). Moreover, income and wealth became even more skewed in favour of those owning Floss-making machinery rather than those who simply worked with it.

A third setback was the revelation by expert medical opinion that Floss might be a prime cause of certain types of cancer which had been increasingly afflicting Innocentians. Once again, however, the pause in development was only temporary. Resources were poured into research into the precise causal relationship between Floss and cancer, and into the provision of hospitalization for those who continued to suffer.

Finally, as is inevitable in a society as sophisticated as Innocentia had become, there was an increase in social tensions. Sociologists are inclined to attribute the mounting crime rate in Innocentia to the rapid rate of change to which its people had been subjected, the undoubtedly hectic pace of life which its dramatic economic development had involved, and more recently, to the stresses of unemployment. Expenditure on police and prisons had to be sharply increased, and on the military as well – a defence against neighbours casting covetous eyes on Innocentian prosperity and knowhow.

Today, Innocentia (or Avaricia as we now know it) is a very rich country indeed with one of the highest per capita income levels in the world. The extent of its remarkable development is shown by the increase in G.N.P. from an original £10,000m. to its present £60,000m. Set out below is a simplified version of its present national output statistics.

	(£m.)
Basic goods	10,000
Floss	20,000
Transport, etc.	10,000
Sales promotion	5,000
Cancer research and hospitals	5,000
Police and prisons	3,000
Defence expenditure	7,000
Total G.N.P.	60,000

An economic miracle if ever there was one. However, Innocentian development is not without its critics. There are those, for example, who argue that its people are not really six times as well off as they were – which is what the figures suggest – because the working week is now twice as long as it used to be – for those lucky enough to have kept their jobs. That certainly seems a fair point. Then again, more puritanical protagonists question whether the introduction of Floss has really contributed to human welfare at all; what they would like to see is a reversion to the original state of happy, laughing Innocentians producing only basic goods. Obviously, this is a highly debatable matter which in the end is up to the Innocentians themselves – but a society without *any* Floss (or its equivalent) might be a very dull one which would not suit most of us.

What is most disturbing about the way in which the growth of Innocentian G.N.P. (or that of other modern industrial economies) is used as an indicator of increased material well-being is what goes into the statistics. Basic goods *plus* Floss only account for £30,000m. of total output. To a very large extent, the other half is made up of expenditure necessary to clean up the mess caused by growth of the Floss sector. It is spending which is an unfortunate and regrettable byproduct of increased production, rather than output which is desired for itself.

Calculations of G.N.P. indiscriminately mix up 'goods' and 'bads' in this way to yield a grand total which therefore has very little meaning at all. To hail an increase in the rate of economic growth as a sign that we are doing well is patently nonsensical – unless we know whether the increased output is of 'goods' or 'bads'. Clearly, if economic growth is to be used to measure development, we must always ask – growth of *what*? Increased output of school buildings? Or space-shuttles? Or ear-muffs? Or aspirins? The answer is very relevant to whether or not we welcome economic growth, but it is a matter which is concealed rather than illuminated by the way in which gross national production figures are presented as a grand hotch-potch of both benefits and drawbacks.

An equally damaging line of criticism of G.N.P. calculations is to inquire about what they leave out. What goes in, since output is measured in terms of prices, is largely that part of output which is bought and sold. But a sizeable proportion of the total consumer satisfaction in an economy may in fact be derived from goods and services which are never 'marketed' in this obvious way. If I grow vegetables in my garden, for example, the result is clearly part of the national output, but not one on which a price is ever put. An even larger element of non-marketed services is the effort of housewives in cleaning, cooking and generally maintaining their homes. And thirdly, there is the 'output' of government social agencies – providing education, hospitals and other facilities for which in a welfare state the customer only partially pays.

To some degree, national income statisticians have overcome these problems. Governmental services *are* included in national income, but they are valued at cost, since there is no obvious price which can be set for them. The flow of satisfaction which an owner-occupier derives from his house is also taken into account, by 'imputing' a notional rent as a measure of that satisfaction. But there are times when national income figures are badly distorted by failure fully to allow for non-marketed elements in national output. During a war, for example, G.N.P. may be growing at a substantial rate. However, part of this growth may come from the increased employment of women who are forced in the process relatively to neglect their own homes. What is recorded in the statistics is their contribution to increased marketed output; what goes unrecorded is the reduction in the amount of housework which they are able to do. (Another reason for increased production during a war period may be that we are all working a good deal harder. But this increased human effort is, once again, something which the national income figures tell us nothing about.)

So far we have been talking only about *gross* national product. A related concept is that of *net* national product, which is the measure of the value of output after allowance has been made for replacing capital which has been worn out during the course of producing that output. Suppose for example, at the beginning of a year, an economy starts off with a stock of factories and machines of £1,000,000m. At the end of the year it has produced a total output of, say, £40,000m. But during the year the value of the original factories and machines has declined by £10,000m. Then the *net* national product is £40,000m. *less* the £10,000m. depreciation of the capital stock. Net national product is the value of output produced while maintaining the value of its capital stock intact.

Numerous technical problems arise for the statisticians in determining the amount which should be deducted for depreciation. These need not concern us here. What should concern us is the narrow coverage of what is conventionally included in the capital stock calculation. Traditionally, capital refers to a stock of *physical* assets – plant, machinery, buildings, roads and such-like. Since they embody scarce resources they have a price, and they can therefore – more or less – be measured.

However, estimating the capital stock of an economy in this way leaves out two very important elements. The first is the quantity of *human* capital which an economy has managed to build up over the years – the ability, aptitude, health, skills and tradition of its people without which no production is possible. Once again the wartime example is relevant. If national output is increased only at the expense of eroding human capital (by neglecting education, impairing health through over-work, etc.) then we really ought to deduct from gross output an appropriate 'human depreciation' figure before calculating net national product. Admittedly, this would be a difficult statistical exercise. But it sometimes makes more sense to hazard a guess about the relatively 'unquantifiable' than to spend a great deal of effort in refining the measurability of the quanti-fiable but less significant parts of the overall sum.

A second major omission from the national accounts is one which has been causing increasing concern since the early 1970s. Economists, principally concerned with resources in finite supply, have traditionally identified a category of 'free goods' as being irrelevant to their particular study. Such goods – air, water (in certain circumstances) and land (in even more par-ticular conditions) – have been labelled 'free' in the sense that they are in sufficiently abundant supply for all who want them to have as much as they like. They therefore create no economic problem.

What has been increasingly recognized in recent years is the extent to which the quantity and quality of these goods is affected by our present scale and processes of production. The problem of *pollution* is seen as more and more urgent and threatening. The fact that certain goods are 'free' means that firms and individuals have not been obliged to take them into account in their production and consumption decisions. That is because the costs which are involved are *external* – they fall on others. Thus the passing tourist who litters the country-side with his rubbish does so at no personal detriment because he is not coming that way again; but his action may mar the enjoyment of countless others – *they* bear the cost. Similarly, the ill-health, inconvenience and loss of amenity caused by a factory chimney belching smoke in the sky never appears in the company's accounts; it is, once again, an external cost borne by the community in the surrounding area.

The costs are nonetheless real. And they are of ever mounting proportions. Air and water may be in abundance, but pure air and clean water are increasingly scarce resources. The social bill which has to be met as a result of the current scale of pollution is difficult to quantify but certainly enormous. What we ought to be doing is to subtract these social costs, this depreciation in our stock of *natural* capital, from the total of national output before arriving at the proper net figure.

Quite staggering estimates have been made, for example, about the costs of air pollution. The chief villains in this respect are power stations and the internal combustion engine. Dirty air helps to destroy not only vegetable life, property and property values but human beings as well. The Council for Environmental Quality has estimated that, taking into account the pollution of air alone, the United States gross national product should be reduced by over ten billion dollars a year. In fact, however, the standard method of G.N.P. calculation involves – as Barbara Ward once pointed out – such irrationalities as 'making no subtraction for days lost or lungs congested' (as a result of air pollution) but 'includes doctors' earnings for putting the troubles right'.[3]

Precisely the same procedure is applied in the case of other pollutants – of water by the discharge of industrial and domestic effluents, of land by the indiscriminate use of pesticides. The original cost of creating the mess is neglected in national product accounts; but what does appear are the costs of cleaning it up. Those costs are then added on to other forms of output to yield a grand G.N.P. total which is used as an index of economic progress.

None of this represents an attack on the desirability of economic growth. After all, between 1979 and 1982 we actually experienced a zero-growth economy. The result was an even more bitter debate about what was to be produced and for whom. Far from solving our economic problems, zero growth seems to have intensified them. For example, take health service 'cuts'. The number of old people in the population, particularly over

3. B. Ward and René Dubos, *Only One Earth*, Penguin Books, 1972, p. 104.

the age of seventy-five, is likely to increase throughout the 1980s. Old people make far heavier demands upon the health service than young people. Hence, despite forecasts of a static total population, more resources will need to be devoted to the health service in the 1980s if even the current standards of service are to be maintained. Yet without economic growth a government committed to cutting public spending cannot 'afford' to increase health service expenditure.

This particular problem is no different from thousands of others arising with zero growth. In such a situation, what is one person's gain must be somebody else's loss. So, if tax rates are reduced for high-income earners, as they were in 1979, it must be the rest of the population who pays for them. If more money is spent on defence, there is less money available for other expenditures. If those in work are to continue to increase their incomes year after year, it must follow that un-employment will have risen or that those out of work will be even poorer than before.

On the other hand, economic growth does not automatically solve such problems. If, after all, the benefits of economic growth go to a tiny minority of high-income earners, or we choose to spend all our extra income on building nuclear missile systems or extra prisons, are ordinary people any better-off?

All this suggests that the growth versus anti-growth debate is couched in terms which themselves make meaningful discussion extremely difficult. Economic growth – which has been regarded as a major *end* of post-war economic policy – turns out, on closer scrutiny, to be an extraordinarily dubious objective. At best, it can be seen as a *means* to the achievement of aims which *are* significant. But in many ways it would be better if we were to forget about growth altogether and set up alternative indicators of economic progress which focus the real issues concealed by the growth index.

'Do we want more growth?' is a question which, after all, it is impossible to answer rationally without a good deal more specific information. We must know, first of all, growth of what? Goods or bads? The composition of output – and, in particular, how a proper balance can be struck between private and public goods – is a vital issue which is seldom brought to the forefront of popular debate. Secondly, we must ask 'Growth for whom?' To which elements in society do the benefits of increased output accrue? Partly, once again, this is a matter of which output is being increased. It also depends on what meanwhile is happening to the distribution of income and wealth. And, thirdly, what costs have been incurred in achieving economic growth? What has been the effect of increased growth on the environment, on amenity, on the pace and quality of working life and leisure?

These are all real world issues and they are hidden away in simplistic concentration on increasing growth as an objective in itself. Certainly, some types of growth *could* serve to solve problems which we all regard as of high priority. But growth can create 'diswelfare' as well as welfare. What above all we must get away from is the idea that growth automatically increases the living standards of the mass of people and the quality of their lives. That there is no such easy equation can be seen from the example of the United States – with a long-term growth performance matched by few other countries. The fact that U.S. output per head is perhaps twice as great as our own does not mean that the majority of American citizens enjoy a standard of living double that of their British counterparts. Behind the impressive economic statistics lies a society which combines the capacity to send men to the moon with the inability to cope with the problems of cities in which it is unsafe to venture out at night. The Great American Dream shows signs of degenerating into a fearful nightmare.

To repeat, the foolishness results from '*single-minded* concentration on *aggregate* production as a social goal'.[4] But how seriously should we take the more extreme view that *any* increased production is undesirable?

The early 1980s have shown that zero growth brings with it problems of its own. In particular, the only way that workers can gain increases in their real after-tax income is for other

4. Ward and Dubos, op. cit.

workers to see a decline in their income or for cuts to be made in public spending. In a zero-growth economy, if we all want to have more video tape recorders, home computers or candy floss, it can only be at the expense of our health service, our education service, our roads, our libraries and so on. Moreover, anti-materialism is generally the province of the 'haves' rather than the 'have-nots'. It is the middle class, appalled at the deterioration of foreign beaches resulting from package-tour holiday-makers, concerned at the congestion and pollution caused by the fact that so many others now enjoy the private motor car, who are most prone to admonish society in general on the evils of materialism. It is observers in the rich countries of the world who tend to extol the virtues of the simple life and urge on poor nations caution in creating a desire for material opulence. With the amount of basic poverty which today exists throughout the world, it is surely premature to deny the real benefits which are still to be derived from increased material wellbeing.

We still need increased output. But it must be of the right sort, directed towards solving the real underlying problems of our society, produced by a technology which is not blatantly wasteful of limited natural resources, and distributed so that all – whether young or old, intelligent or mentally retarded, fit or handicapped, white or black – share the benefit equitably. Instead, sadly we are moving towards a more divided society where the 'haves' and the 'have-nots' are becoming increasingly distanced. On a world scale, that becomes even more disgracefully apparent.

16

The Poorest of the Poor

The inequities and distortions which exist within affluent economies are totally dwarfed by the division of the world into rich and poor nations. It is in this broad international setting that questions of 'what most people regard as urgent and menacing' are of the most profound importance. It is at this level that the issues which we have been discussing are posed with a stark and disturbing clarity. The continued existence of poverty and world inequality on their present scale represent *the* most pressing economic problem of our times. Incredibly, it is a matter to which mainstream economics has devoted relatively little attention.

The present economic system has resulted in the evolution of a 'development gap' of gigantic proportions, a gap which year by year is widening rather than narrowing. While a small group of nations wrestle with the problems of gross affluence, the majority of the world's population live in poverty and deprivation almost unimaginable for those in rich countries. How has this absurd and morally intolerable situation come about?

World inequality stems from basically the same causes as those defects of our own economy which have been the subject so far. They are the outcome of ostensibly 'fair' and 'free' market forces working within a framework which is itself imperfect and inequitable. Unregulated, the code of the market is little more than the law of the jungle in which benefits accrue only to those strong enough to seize them – whatever the initial source of their strength. The present development gap is the product of a century and a half of the disequalizing operation of such market forces.

In its broadest terms, the blame can be laid at the door of 'free trade' – the doctrine that it is best for nations, like individuals, to specialize according to their particular advantages and to exchange their surpluses without impediment from import duties, quotas and other 'barriers' to the free movement of goods in the international market. The original proponents of the free-trade theory argued that this maximizing of international trade was the way to secure the greatest *world* welfare – and that in the process all would benefit. Whether an economy was advanced or backward, industrial or heavily dependent on agriculture, rich or poor – *all* the partners in the free-trade enterprise would gain. It would pay them all to open their doors to the freest interchange.

Take, for example, an extreme case of two countries, one of which could produce all goods more efficiently than the other. Surely, in this case at least, there is nothing for either of them in the notion of specialization and trade? On the contrary, argued the free traders. The more efficient should still specialize in output where its advantage over the other is the greatest. If country X produces both industrial and primary goods more cheaply than country Y, but its advantage is most marked in industrial goods, then it will pay it to concentrate on industrial production, increase output accordingly – and in the process secure its primary products more cheaply through exports than it could by producing them itself. The less efficient Y, meanwhile, will obviously have benefited through being able to import cheaper industrial goods.

What could be fairer? Certainly, David Ricardo and the others who helped to give birth to the free-trade doctrine in the nineteenth century saw it as a way, not only of increasing the size of the world economic cake, but also ensuring that all who participated in its baking got a bigger slice. How then can it now be denigrated as an engine for perpetuating and widening international economic inequalities?

First of all, the outcome of free trade very much depends on the initial starting-point of the parties concerned. And by the beginning of the nineteenth century, an initial inequality had already emerged. A handful of European economies and economies originally peopled from Europe had begun a break-through to modern industrial growth. Moreover, they had established a political dominance over much of the rest of the world which enabled them to impose on it a trade pattern of their own choosing. It was they who would concentrate on manufactured goods. Others would specialize in the production of raw materials. To ensure that this was so, the metropolitan powers when necessary destroyed industries in the subordinate territories, as in the classic case of Indian textiles, or tried to prevent their emergence (though unsuccessfully in the case of the American colonies).

Trade was therefore between unequals. The Ricardian claim that all would gain *might* still be true. But how would the gains be divided between those taking part in international trade? Everything suggests that a state of 'free' competition between unequals can be exploited more successfully by the stronger partner. Although both may gain, it will be the stronger which gains most. The rich may get richer and the poor may get richer, but the rich get richer at a faster rate. And that is what has happened. The classical doctrine, adopting a world view, neglected the question of how the undoubted benefits of inter-national trade would be shared out. This is typical of tradi-tional economic theory: to try to separate matters of economic efficiency (which can be discussed in objective terms) from those of distribution (which involve making value-judgements). But obviously, from the point of view of the poorer nations, distribution is the vital issue. Their concern is not so much with the size of the world cake as with how big a slice of it comes their way. It may well be the case that by having only limited trade they could do a great deal better.

Moreover, the division of labour which was established historically between rich and poor countries was a deeply unfair one. It may at first sight seem obviously sensible that countries should specialize along complementary lines. Manufacturers need raw materials, foodstuffs and primary producing countries need manufactures. But the demand and supply conditions for manufactures and primary products are very different. As world incomes grow, it may be true that demand for both industrial and primary products increases. But as we get richer we spend a smaller proportion of our incomes on foodstuffs. The growth in world demand will be much greater for industrial products. And on the supply side, not only are the opportunities for applying technical change in mass production much greater in manufacturing industry than in agriculture; industrial countries also have the ability to produce synthetic substitutes for natural raw materials.

It may well be the case that some of the countries currently specializing in primary production would have had a comparative advantage in manufactures had they been allowed to develop in that direction. It may still be the case that *potential* comparative advantage suggests a quite different pattern of output from the present one. But, at least in a free-trade situation, it is impossible for poor countries ever to get their infant industries off the ground in face of competition from established producers already enjoying the economies of scale. What is more, the present industrial nations not only have the advantage *now*; they are also in the position, by spending more on research and development into new products and processes, cumulatively to widen that lead over the years.

It is no wonder that underdeveloped countries label an organization like G.A.T.T. (General Agreement on Tariffs and Trade) as essentially a 'rich man's club'. G.A.T.T. has worked throughout the post-war period for liberalization of trade on the principle of reciprocity: that countries should match each others' cuts in trade restrictions and extend these concessions to all other members of the international trading community. But if the development gap is ever to be reduced, this will not do at all for the developing countries. What *they* need is the right to protect themselves against competition from the more advanced economies, while at the same time enjoying free access to the markets of the rich. Indeed what is called for is not merely equal terms of exchange but positive discrimination in favour of the poorer nations.

Free-trade theory, which purported to be objective economics of universal applicability, is nothing of the sort. It was the product of thinking in white, nineteenth-century, relatively advanced capitalist economies. Although the inventors of the doctrine may not have realized it, it was heavily biased in favour of the rich industrial nations. And it continues to be so today.

Similar effects follow from other aspects of international economic liberalization. For example, the policy-makers lay much stress on the importance of allowing free movement of capital, labour and technical knowledge between economies. Theory again suggests that such mobility will be generally beneficial. But in practice it is once more a case of the poor being the relative losers from such transfers.

For, in fact, perfect mobility would often lead to perverse movements – from poor economies to rich ones. Many wealth-holders in underdeveloped economies would like nothing better than to switch their capital to safer and more profitable use in rich countries – and they often succeed in illicitly doing so. Labour, when immigration laws allow it, moves in the same direction. But unfortunately, it is generally that skilled labour – doctors, nurses and graduates – which the poor countries can least afford to lose. The same mechanism of cumulative causation which works to create personal and regional inequalities within a country also perpetuates and widens international disparities.

Even when capital and technical knowledge *are* transferred from advanced to underdeveloped economies, it is generally into narrow sectors. The modern, industrial urban areas are those which are most attractive to both private foreign investment and official aid. The result is that foreign capital and technology, instead of spreading economic development, more often accentuate the basically *dualistic* nature of underdeveloped economies. Output from the modern sector kills off traditional industries. But, being based on the economics of the rich West, it is a technology which uses a lot of capital and economizes on labour – which is what poor economies happen to have in embarrassing abundance. It therefore adds to the massive unemployment which is already the most desperate of the problems of the Third World and which is bound to become still worse – the product, not just of population explosion but also of misguided educational and wage policies which have led to a futile and fatal drift from the rural sector. Moreover, not only is modern technology rather inefficient, because it is alien and inappropriate for those at a different stage of development; foreign investment is also essentially homeward-looking, involving an unwanted outflow of profits, interest and dividends.

Altogether, then, the cards are heavily stacked against the poorer two-thirds of the world. And in their policies on trade, aid and investment the rich few show little inclination to bring about any change in this fundamentally unjust state of affairs.

The case of underdeveloped countries highlights not only the issue of inequality, but also the absurdity of using increases in gross national product as a measure of economic progress. Judged by this dubious criterion, the record of the Third World has often been distinctly impressive. Historically unprecedented growth rates, averaging 4 per cent in the 1960s, for example, might suggest that underdeveloped economies had finally 'taken off'. But quite apart from the fact that the growth performance of the rich economies was even better during these years, and that a good deal of increased output in poor countries was swallowed up by rapidly increasing population, the nonsense of equating growth with progress is even more patently obvious in the case of underdeveloped economies than it is in the affluent West.

For once we look behind the growth rates, what do we find in a typical underdeveloped country? In the first place, it will be suffering from unemployment and underemployment on a scale which, although difficult to measure precisely because of the inadequacy of statistics, far exceeds the worst ever endured in the advanced industrial economies. It is even more chronic than unemployment in the rich countries and cannot be solved by Keynesian techniques of pumping in more demand

– which once worked in the rich countries because capital as well as labour was lying idle or capable of being increased. In the poor world, there is no spare capital to be drawn into production. The problem of unemployment, already of alarming proportions, is persistently deteriorating as high rates of population increase throw millions of young people each year onto a labour market which, with present policies and techniques, cannot conceivably absorb them.

Moreover, if income and wealth are very unequally distributed in rich countries, such disparities are even more marked in the underdeveloped world. Widening inequalities abound not just between individuals but also between regions and between town and countryside, with a relatively prosperous urban modernity superimposed on an impoverished traditional rural sector. It is not surprising that the resulting pattern of output is one which can satisfy the demands of the few for air conditioners, motor cars and refrigerators while leaving millions to suffer from serious malnutrition.

Concentrating on the growth index conceals all these vital considerations. Development means more than growth. However difficult to measure, it must have a qualitative as well as a quantitative dimension. Achieving development is not simply a matter of manipulating certain key economic variables within a given socio-economic context. It involves changing the context itself and basically transforming attitudes and institutions. Above all, it requires the political will to overcome the many anti-developmental interests which exist both inside and outside poor countries.

Recently, the Brandt Report[1] has again highlighted the plight of the Third World, and emphasized the global implications of two-thirds of the world living in conditions of poverty. These are not only economic but political. Poverty and inequality, it was agreed, led to political destabilization and an increased likelihood of war. The report stressed the links between the rich 'North' and the poor 'South', through trade in food, commodities and manufactured goods, through financial markets

1. Published as *North–South: A Programme for Survival*, Pan Books, 1980.

and through inflation and employment. Such was their interdependence, it claimed, the rich could solve their own problems only by giving greater assistance to the poor.

But the Brandt Report failed to achieve acceptance of a new political outlook. Discussion of whether or not its recommendations would provide a solution to Third World problems has remained academic. For example, central to the report was the proposal that there should be a major transfer of resources from the North to the South. The British government's response to this call was typical of many others in reasserting the importance of foreign aid and a longstanding commitment to work towards an aid target of 0·7 per cent of G.N.P.[2] And yet within a week of the release of the Brandt Commission Report, the government had announced a significant cut in the aid budget. Unfortunately, it must be recognized that the rich industrialized nations of the world are *not* going to make any significant sacrifices to help the poorer nations of the world. The implication of this is that Third World countries need to define their own aims and objectives and find their own solutions to development. What is currently happening is that the developed nations of the world are imposing *their* aims and objectives on the Third World but are failing to provide the means for their achievement. The result is the absurd pattern of development which leads to a Western lifestyle for a small minority and further impoverishment for the vast majority.

We have seen that even in an economy such as our own, economic policies may be severely constrained by international factors. How free then are present underdeveloped countries to exercise a conscious option about the type of development they follow? Or are they doomed to a pursuit of economic growth regardless of its consequences?

Given present levels of poverty in the Third World, the question of whether they should try to achieve material or non-

2. 'The Brandt Commission Report', memorandum prepared by the Foreign and Commonwealth Office for the Overseas Development Sub-committee of the Foreign Affairs Committee, July 1980.

material ends is an unreal one. For the time being they simply have to concern themselves with increasing output. The immediate issue is how that should be done. Only at a later stage does the matter of how far they go along the road of material advancement become relevant.

Many of them, however, already seem set on what looks like the typical growth pattern pioneered by the early nineteenth-century developers. Broadly, it can be characterized as a sacrificial process in which jam tomorrow can be won only at the price of regrettable but inevitable hardship today. Inequality and unbalanced development are seen as the necessary cost of achieving the breakthrough to higher standards of living for all at a later stage. It is a harsh and painful type of development based on essentially unplanned private enterprise. But it may be working in cases like Hong Kong, Taiwan, South Korea. These countries have suffered a considerable loss of national identity in the process. But, nonetheless, basic changes have been brought about, with the mass of people involved in the dynamics of change – although they may not all be beneficiaries.

But for many other countries, their close involvement with the western world through trade, investment and aid has succeeded only in creating pockets of capitalist activity without disturbing the underlying social fabric. (The idea that the modern enclave will ultimately absorb the traditional sector of the economy seems far less plausible than the view that they will turn out to be 'mutually poisoning'.) What is worrying about this group is that they are economies in which all the hardships of capitalist development are imposed without any guarantee that its ultimate fruits will be realized. What is also disturbing is the fact that few of them appear to have consciously opted for this particular type of development. In many ways they ostensibly try to resist it – with declarations of socialist values often built into their very constitutions and considerable lip-service paid to the ideal of planning. But, in practice, their enmeshment with western markets, western ideas and technology means that this is no more than an ideological façade.

Only a few have from the outset determined that their course of development should be a radically different one. China, Burma and Tanzania provide examples of the very diverse alternatives which are open. China is probably big enough to get away with it on its own. Burma, because of its anti-materialist emphasis, can also perhaps afford isolationism. But it is the Tanzanias of the world which are in real difficulty. Aiming from the start at an egalitarian rural development based on an appropriate technology, Tanzania's smallness and desperate poverty make it hard for it to remain independent of the outside world. But it is also difficult for it to secure the help it needs on terms which will not distort the philosophy of its development.

The chasm which separates the rich countries from the poor is merely a magnification of the processes at work within our own economy. The mechanisms which create such basic economic injustices are the same. And perhaps we shall only be able to contribute towards solving the problem of international inequality if we put our own house in order. For the present, our lack of interest in such wider issues simply mirrors the decreasing concern that we show to weaker members of our own society. We neglect both at our peril.

Index